THE FUTURE OF BROADCASTING

Also by Richard Hoggart

AUDEN
THE USES OF LITERACY
W. H. AUDEN
W. H. AUDEN: A Selection (*editor*)
TEACHING LITERATURE
THE CRITICAL MOMENT
HOW AND WHY DO WE LEARN
THE WORLD IN 1984
GUIDE TO THE SOCIAL SCIENCES
TECHNOLOGY AND SOCIETY
ESSAYS ON REFORM
YOUR SUNDAY PAPER (*editor*)
SPEAKING TO EACH OTHER (2 volumes)
ONLY CONNECT (The Reith Lectures)
AN IDEA AND ITS SERVANTS

Also by Janet Morgan

THE HOUSE OF LORDS AND THE LABOUR
   GOVERNMENT, 1964–70
THE DIARIES OF A CABINET MINISTER 1964–70
   (3 volumes) (*editor*)
THE BACKBENCH DIARIES OF RICHARD CROSSMAN
   1951–63 (*editor*)

THE FUTURE OF BROADCASTING

Essays on authority, style and choice

Edited by

RICHARD HOGGART
and
JANET MORGAN

© The Foundations of Broadcasting Policy 1982

First published 1982 by
THE MACMILLAN PRESS LTD
London and Basingstoke
Companies and representatives
throughout the world

ISBN 0 333 28848 3

Printed in Hong Kong

To the memory of
Colin Cherry
a pioneer in the
study of communications

Contents

Introduction

There are many conferences about broadcasting every year; and many of them cover the same ground. What made the Leeds Castle conference of May 1980 distinctive was its unusual and, at first glance, formal-seeming theme. It was about 'The Foundations of Broadcasting Policy', and so about 'authority' first of all (Who sets the systems up? On what criteria and with what aims? What *is* the exact 'authority' of those who, whether as members of a supervisory board or as full-time professionals, then operate the systems? What is their responsibility to their audiences?).

The nature of 'authority' and of the way it is exercised in turn decides the 'style' (temper, texture, feel, air, tone, manner) of each broadcasting system. How does that show itself in British broadcasting, in what is not done and said as much as in what is?

'Authority' and 'style' together define the 'choices' put before the audiences in any one place and at any one time. And here there comes in that whole range of questions about the responsiveness of the professionals to their audiences' needs and wishes and, just as important, of their freedom to experiment and explore needs and tastes still unknown to many in those audiences.

These were the three interlocking themes of the meeting. They produced discussions of exceptional interest. But transcripts of discussions are almost invariably as dull as last week's newspapers; so we decided against reproducing them. Instead, Janet Morgan has written a chapter, to accompany the background papers in this book, on the main themes of the discussion, its movement and shape, as they emerged over the two and a half days. Richard Hoggart's final chapter is a tidied-up version of some closing remarks inspired by the meeting.

An enterprise such as this has several parents. Yet everyone involved with this one would want to give first credit to the late Professor Colin Cherry, who was in from the start and who expressed his interest in the most tangible way — by giving a substantial part of his Marconi Research Award towards the costs. He knew that cancer might not let him attend the meeting itself. So it was. He died only a few weeks before.

A great debt is also due to the Hosa Bunka Foundation of Japan. They were imaginative enough to think a conference so far away, and in such a different setting from their own, worth their financial support. For good measure, the Japanese representative at the conference introduced some very pertinent comments to the discussion itself from his unusual perspective.

We are also greatly in debt to the Board of the Leeds Castle Foundation and especially to its most hospitable Chairman, Lord Geoffrey-Lloyd. It would be hard to find a more agreeable ivory tower for a hard spell of thinking.

The proceedings themselves were steered with his usual remarkable combination of courtesy and firmness by Lord Boyle. We have some idea how hard-pressed he is and therefore all the more appreciate his readiness to spare so much time.

Although he will not like our saying so, the main begetter of the meeting and of this book was Kenneth Lamb, then in charge of the BBC's research interests. Against formidable obstacles, not only financial, he pursued the idea until it was finally fulfilled. Through him we thank also the BBC itself for substantial help in kind.

Finally, Kenneth Lamb was very ably assisted in all the complex preparations by Doreen Stephens and Lesley Mills.

R. H., J. M.

1 Shirley Williams

My presence at this symposium as a contributor puzzles me. After all, the Annan *Committee on the Future of Broadcasting*, quoting the work of Professor Burns,[1] agreed with him that loyalty to the ideal of public service in the BBC had given way to loyalty to the concept of professionalism. It is well known that politicians are the last of the amateurs and generalists, those who aspire to know everything and consequently know nothing. Over a century ago, the prescient Robert Louis Stevenson said that 'politics is perhaps the only profession for which no preparation is thought necessary'.[2] That is still largely true today. What I have learned I have learned in the fascinating and bruising school of the experience of government. As far as broadcasting is concerned, anyone who has read the blue and white papers produced by various governments at various times, would not regard them as classic works on the subject. Perhaps I am here as some last dim echo of the Reithian tradition? So be it. I shall carry the banner of public service for you.

Let me begin with a flourish of trumpets for the BBC. The BBC is unquestionably going through a troubled time. It has been afflicted with substantial cuts and they have been unpopular and much criticised. Certainly they would have been criticised wherever they fell, but the excision of whole orchestras and large chunks of educational broadcasting is peculiarly agonising for those of us who admire the BBC's great achievements in these fields. Furthermore, I get the strong impression that there wasn't a great deal of consultation. It is perfectly true that consultation can be an excuse for inactivity, but any organisation whose members and supporters actually care a lot about it have some right to be heard. The BBC no longer has the resources it needs to exploit the exciting new technical developments in communications, technical developments which open out vast potential for more, and more ambitious, programmes, for instant information, and for the transformation of the 'information industry'. Unable to pay competitive salaries, the BBC is losing some of its talented young producers to the independent service and to broadcasting companies abroad, especially in the United States. The BBC also lacks the resources to allow it to exploit existing technologies fully, though a modicum of new equipment has recently improved matters. There is also the problem of opposition from the unions where new developments could reduce manning levels, though light portable equipment is already being used by foreign television companies and by ITV, which has run into trouble over it. There seems to have been some decline in the BBC's standards of presentation: there are more and more unsynchronised shots, there are stumbling bulletins sometimes actually approaching incomprehensibility (as at moments in the commentary on the Iranian Embassy siege). The missing button and the odd patch show, however excellent the cloth.

But I do mean it all the same — the flourish of trumpets with which I began. The BBC is indubitably the best broadcasting company in the world. Its reputation internationally is unparalleled, for quality, for sensitivity, for creativity, and not least for truthfulness. It was the late Adlai Stevenson, the most urbane and charming of American Presidential candidates (they don't grow them like that any more) who once commented on some sensational tale, 'a lie runs round the world while the truth is pulling on its boots'. The BBC I would submit, by consistency and determination, has caught up. In his book, *The Third Floor Front*, Hugh Carleton Greene[3] reminded us of the many Germans under the Third Reich who listened to the BBC because it reported Allied defeats as well as Allied victories; it would be wrong to say that the facts were entirely sacred; they clearly were not. But nevertheless they were much less defiled by the BBC than by other national broadcasting corporations in those years. Afghans, Czechs, Chileans, have all praised the BBC for the accuracy of its news accounts of what happened in their own countries. Very recently the BBC's Washington correspondent learned about the American attempt to rescue the hostages in Tehran, and learned it from a White House source who clearly wanted the BBC to have the news first. That kind of international standing is very precious. It would be short-sighted and mistaken to let the BBC External News Services slip towards propaganda. Every last tin-pot broadcasting station, anywhere in the world, produces propaganda. It does not inspire loyalty in the long run. (I mention, incidentally, radio, not television because the BBC's television news does seem rather parochial sometimes. I don't believe the same is true of radio.)

I hope that ITV will forgive me if I say that I believe its marked improvement in the last fifteen years has been assisted by the existence of, and competition from, the BBC. The two organisations have benefited each other: Independent Television forced the BBC to unstuff, if that's the right verb for ceasing to be a bit stuffy. The need to compete has been a very useful argument against the critics and pressure groups who would like the BBC to be unrelievedly and gloomily high-minded. On the other hand, the tradition of public broadcasting has made it easier for the independent contractors to resist control by advertisers over programmes, and has made it easier to get acceptance of constructive supervision by the Independent Broadcasting Authority. Both broadcasting systems try to cover the whole spectrum of interests in the programmes they produce. Both make programmes that will appeal to a majority or a very large part of the viewing and listening population, and sometimes it may be a lowest common denominator of soap opera or slush. But the sour warning of Norman Collins, one of ITV's founding fathers, that 'If you gave the people what they wanted, the programmes would be deplorable',[4] has simply not been borne out. Broadcasters have discovered that some of the time, even much of the time, majorities are made up of minorities; that people are transformed and invigorated by their own special interest or fascinations or skill; that Orwell's description of the British people as 'this nation of flower-lovers and stamp collectors, pigeon fanciers, amateur carpenters, coupon snippers, darts players and crossword puzzle fans'[5] is nearer the truth than the image of some amorphous unmotivated mass.

So let me pay tribute to what broadcasters have done for this country of absorbed minorities. Let me say thank you for making me for one burst out laughing over the washing-up at *Not The Nine O'Clock News*, which I think is in the great tradition of BBC TV humour but able to be uproarious without the viciousness of some of its predecessors; and thanks to radio for *Week Ending* which is the seed of the whole idea. Thanks for the horse jumpers and the gymnasts and *Match of the Day* and snooker. It all goes on a bit long for me, especially the rhythmic obsessive horses, but it is marvellous camera work and excellent commentary. Our sports reporting has a great advantage over American competitors: the commentators don't talk all the time as if the viewers couldn't see pictures. ITV deserves credit too, for *News at Ten* and for the majestic tranquillity of *The English Garden* and for Granada's tough documentaries, just to name three. And who could forget the radio, which has educated thousands of us in music through the modulated tones of the marvellously well informed Patricia Hughes, and which explores the anatomy of politics, both national and international, in a way that I think television is only just beginning to learn.

Let me look for a moment more closely at the current pains and strains of broadcasting. The sadness of this austere time is that this reputation, this record and this talent cannot flourish as they should as the explosion of information and communications occurs which is now made imminent by technological advances. Britain may be deindustrialising, and the industrial news charts show that decline. But it is better placed than almost any other country in the world to benefit from the growth of what is now called the quaternary sector, the information/education/software segment of the economy. Our basic school education is good and standards have been rising. Our universities and polytechnics have a deserved international reputation, and some of them are in the international first rank at a time when many Continental European universities have been knocked sideways by student troubles and by half-digested reforms. The library system is good, and the British Library has been in the vanguard of computerised reference and access systems with international links. The coming of micro-electronics and optic fibre communications systems could precipitate us into the post-industrial world, with the great additional benefit of the best methods of handling news, information and knowledge which have yet been devised.

The present government's expenditure cuts, however, are unselective. They will hit research, including research into essential new technologies like micro-electronics. They will affect the standards of education and reduce the amount of training for new skills and new techniques. They have already swept away the proposed new British Library and made the education here of overseas students prohibitively expensive. It is sad to see the seedcorn scattered.

In his Fleming Memorial Lecture,[6] Sir Michael Swann said that 'quite a lot of the £130 million, in fact £90 million, will be found by deferring or abandoning planned new development in the BBC', and he pointed out, very fairly, that the BBC was not being asked to bear a disproportionate level of cuts. But how often is it the new developments that have to be abandoned? Every Minister knows it is easier to cut capital programmes than to cut current revenues, to sacrifice the future as distinct from the present. In the long run, however, the price of obsolescence is very high. It isn't surprising to learn that Britain has the oldest capital stock of any industrialised nation, a fact that goes further to explain our poor productivity than seems to me to be publicly realised.

The Annan Report,[7] and I think it's a very good report, described broadcasting as exclusive, transient and one-way, and then went on to point out that each of these limitations is about to vanish. The coming of the geostationary satellite next year, the dramatic cheapening of video tapes and the arrival of video discs, and the possibility of two-way access through individual terminals, open up a new world to broadcasters. But like other new worlds, this one has its perils. The BBC is crippled by inadequate finance. Everyone agrees that the licence fee is much the most satisfactory way to raise the BBC's revenue, since it is at one remove from the government, makes the BBC independent of advertising, and underlines the broadcasting system's accountability through Parliament to the public, and not to the executive.[8] The trouble is, as we all know, that governments dislike putting up the licence fee, especially near an election. So either the licence fee should be based on a quinquennium, perhaps with a certain provisional quality for the last two years, and with an inbuilt review for inflation; or it should be indexed for several years at a time, with the possibility of special additional funds for unforeseen developments. As Sir Michael Swann pointed out in his lecture, it is important to try to arrange some kind of payment by instalments, perhaps by linking licence payments to quarterly electricity bills. I don't myself see why the rental companies shouldn't add the appropriate monthly sum to the rental, and be responsible for collecting the licence fee. This could be complemented by a requirement that no-one could buy a television set without presenting a valid licence to the seller, who would record its number. Finally, it does seem right to me that both broadcasting systems should contribute towards the cost of collection and of chasing offenders, as the Annan Report suggested.

The licence question has become even more critical because of the award of the fourth channel to ITV. In a situation where there is no incomes policy, this could pose a serious threat to the BBC. It is now clear that the ITV system will be in a position to offer more competitive salaries to the talent that is available for broadcasting, in one form or another, and that the fact that there is no incomes policy means that the differential between ITV and BBC staff is

likely to widen. Paradoxically it is very much in the interest of the
BBC that there should be an incomes policy; if there isn't, then the
burden and responsibility on the government to link the licence fee
to inflation and beyond becomes even more central and even more
grave than it was when we first discussed this matter in 1978 and in
1979.

The prospect of Pay Television, or subscription TV, is a mixed
one for the reasons that were advanced by the Pilkington
Committee[9] when it came out in opposition to the whole idea. I fear
that a BBC starved for licence money will be driven into making its
best and newest productions for the cable subscription services on
the grounds that this will help to finance better off-air programmes.
But the temptation to provide the evidently better service to
subscribers will be real, and could threaten the quality and integrity
of public broadcasting. The analogy with the National Health
Service worries me. Public broadcasting, like a public health
service, can stand an element of direct competition, given that both
have to meet certain standards. But the existence of competition
which is not openly recognised, within the system itself, is a much
more damaging business. I would like to see cable used entirely for
local and community television and perhaps for additional open-
access programmes, thereby relieving the pressure from special-
interest groups wanting to make their own broadcasts. Pay
television will, I think, be very dangerous indeed unless it is tightly
controlled; I grant that it could help our ailing film industry and
Tony Smith will make the point if I don't, but it could very easily
shut off the greatest sporting and artistic events from those who are
simply unable to pay.

Finance is obviously at the heart of the BBC's problems; in an
opposite sense it is at the heart of the ITV's worries as well. But all
broadcasters, whether independent or public service, are involved
in the shopworn and unresolved problem, the dichotomy of
creativity and responsibility, which will be with us always. First,
then, the producer is at the centre of broadcasting, and if
broadcasting is to be exciting and stirring and inspired, both he or
she and his or her bosses have to be willing to take risks. 'It is what
people are . . . that determines the value of the output', Grace
Wyndham Goldie wrote in her splendid book, *Facing the Nation*.[10]
The public does not get used to new ideas or new approaches
overnight; indeed, as Hugh Carleton Greene pointed out, new ideas
may elicit public hostility. The power of producers is obviously

enormous in any creative organisation which does not indulge in pre-censorship. The whole organisation basks in producers' success and trembles when they err. In the days when the BBC was the only broadcasting system in Britain, there was, I gather, an internal discipline based on certain expectations of behaviour and even *de facto* codes of practice which young producers absorbed as they rose up the Corporation's ladder. In the early years, immense attention was given to appointments. Grace Wyndham Goldie once told me that she personally attended the appointments boards even for the lowest production posts and regarded this as being among the most important responsibilities that she had.

But now the young producer can move across to the independent sector, and into a variety of contracting companies there. Even within the BBC, radio and television offer very different careers. And I suspect rather less minute attention is paid by senior executives to the choice of production assistants than when the BBC was a smaller organisation. Yet the creation of an internal set of values or principles comprising honesty in reporting, integrity about editing, loyalty to providing the fairest representation of a situation that can be devised — or for that matter of an author's or composer's intentions — this is much the most satisfactory, indeed the only satisfactory guarantee of a balance between the demands of creativity and the restraints of responsibility. It is much more difficult now, when there is a plurality of broadcasting outlets, when the BBC itself is much more sectionalised and much less monolithic than in Reith's day, and when society itself questions even the most orthodox of values.

The most sensitive aspect of this dichotomy between creativity and responsibility arises in news, documentaries and foreign affairs. What can I say about the scars left behind by the unshown film of Carrickmore[11] or by *Death of a Princess*?[12] Obviously programmes on such controversial topics must be made in a free society. For one thing, the media are a vital safeguard against corruption, atrocities or excess by the authorities. There is a duty to provide information, most of all where human life or liberty are involved. But in such sore areas, the broadcasters also have an obligation, and it is to make as sure as they possibly can that the reporting is balanced and objective. Nor should broadcasters forget that extremists and terrorists are parasitical on publicity. Publicity feeds them. So this too must be borne in mind. The temptation for sensationalism must be resisted.

More disturbing is the emerging fashion for 'faction', which seems to describe, to me at least, *Death of a Princess*. Just as newspapers shouldn't mix comments with news reports, so broadcasters ought not to run fact and fiction together. There are examples of faction in politics, obviously; indeed there is an element of faction in Richard Crossman's famous diaries.[13] But at least others could respond and correct what was written. It was on the record and it was permanent. The transience of television and radio make faction much more damaging in these media even than in newspapers. In my view, the line between fact and fiction, drama and documentary, must be clear and must be held. Clear labelling of programmes would be valuable here, indicating for instance what is reconstructed as distinct from what is real. Faction is, simply, indefensible. And broadcasters sometimes need defenders.

There are more obscure borders between what is acceptable and what is not. How far should a producer be allowed to contrive a situation to add emphasis or to make a point? In my view only if it represents what actually happened as faithfully as possible. For instance, I don't believe the sequence in the film about Faraday School in *Panorama*, shown in March 1977, where children were shown smoking, was on the right side of the border. The same holds for the editing of film or the spoken word; what is left should be representative of what was there originally. One of the reasons for the great and lasting row about *Yesterday's Men*, the programme on the Opposition made shortly after Labour's defeat in 1970, was that the purpose of the film was misrepresented to the politicians who took part in it, and the editing was unfair. I recall for instance that the late Anthony Crosland appeared to own most of an elegant London terrace plus the public park behind.

One of the most difficult balances to strike in broadcasting political and current affairs programmes is between two values, both important: the pursuit of truth and the building-up of trust. Governments and individual politicians try to hide what is to their discredit. It is the job of reporters and of broadcasters to find out what is really going on. The Watergate scandal is the most notorious example, but in Britain the Poulson case (after some delay), the Stonehouse case and the Thorpe story were all unearthed by the media. Since Watergate, American newspapers have been obsessed by scandal, chasing every scent like bloodhounds, and there are plenty of trails to follow.

But there is the other value, and that's trust. Democracies die unless people have some trust in those they elect to represent them and to lead them. People in public life must deserve trust. Yet what they do to deserve it gets very little coverage. Politics, particularly in central government, is still quite remarkably uncorrupt in this country. In my entire political career, in which I have at various times had considerable discretionary power over prices and profits, mergers and monopolies, as well as powers of appointment, I have never once been approached by anyone with even the faintest hint of either a bribe or a favour. The only time I was so approached was long ago in West Africa, when a notorious financier, who later served a long prison term, pressed a crumpled £5 note into my hand, which seemed to me a rather contemptuously low valuation, so I gave it back. Nor do broadcasters adequately reveal the colossal pressures that politicians confront, sometimes from their own supporters, and sometimes from pressure groups or special interests, pressures that many politicians actually combat with courage. I often feel that politics, at least on television, is dealt with very superficially; the 'web of corporate power' is not much explored. This is of course partly because television and radio people are pretty ignorant of politics: they know what they read, but they have little knowledge of political structures and little feel for a political atmosphere. I hope the advent of the new House of Commons Select Committees, covering the work of the several departments of state, will enable television, as well as radio, to explore more thoroughly the commercial, professional and industrial interests that try to shape and influence policy. In this context I think the new Radio 4 programme *Inside Parliament* has made a very good start.

One of the other reasons for tension between politicians and the broadcasting media is that the image and the reality are constantly confused. Television personalises politics; indeed it creates an illusion of a personal relationship between the viewer and the politician concerned, one in which the viewer feels that he or she knows the politician intimately. Hence television has vastly increased the invasion of privacy of public figures. The best public men and women I know are not actors and actresses; they think and feel and worry about what they do and about the decisions that they have to make. Yet through television they become images — actors in some drama called politics — and the fact that they are real men and women operating in a real world is easily obscured. Hence the personal attacks that some of them have to endure seem permissible because they are somehow not thought to be real. I recall that incredible slur on the Prime Minister of the day in *That was the Week that Was* — and I quote — 'If you see his lips move, he must be lying'. I had a young Polish student leader visiting me at the time that that programme was put out. He burst into my room saying 'You must escape, there is about to be a coup'. He couldn't believe that anyone would dare publicly to attack the Prime Minister in such terms, unless that Prime Minister was absolutely certain to fall from office within the next few days. I agree that it should be possible in a democracy and it is. But it isn't costless, either for broadcasters or for the fabric of democracy itself, which does depend on trust. Producers should occasionally remember Shylock's cry: 'If you prick us, do we not bleed? If you tickle us, do we not laugh? If you poison us, do we not die? And if you wrong us, shall we not seek revenge?'

I am concerned about the impact of television on politics for three reasons. One I have mentioned, which is the intense personalisation of politics. The Cabinet system in Britain helps to modify it a bit, since the Prime Minister is not the sole figure on the stage. But not much. The 'politician as actor' emphasises appearance, age, voice, recognisability. Hence the success of a Ronald Reagan, for instance, a man who knows how to capitalise on exactly such characteristics. Hence too the stumble that haunts Edmund Muskie, his all-to-human reaction to the Press campaign about his wife, when he broke down in the 1972 Presidential primary campaign, a reaction that did not fit the politician-actor's role of strong silent statesman. The emphasis on appearance and style exemplified in that experience of Senator Muskie downgrades knowledge and experience. The emphasis on name recognition downgrades a person's attitude to issues, his political stance. And in the end it helps to fragment the political parties and the political system, as is happening now, in the United States.

Television, secondly, underlines adversary politics, the Westminster model of confrontation. It is an easy formula to copy on the small screen, adapts itself to the short time spans of television, and satisfies very simply the requirement that broadcasting should balance the time given to each major party's views. Furthermore, MPs take to the ring cheerfully, slogging it out with their opposite numbers like so many sparring partners. But it isn't a subtle model, and it tends to eliminate shades of opinion within parties and between individual politicians. It does not lend itself to the politics of either conciliation or accommodation. Above all, it concentrates on current issues and current differences, yet medium- and long-term political issues may be of crucial importance, as I believe they are now. But they get short shrift from television. Admittedly, life isn't easy for the broadcasting authorities either. When the country is broadly united and politics is played on a keyboard of consensus, the authorities do not have too hard a time. Their judgements of balance and impartiality will be broadly accepted. It is when politics become fiercely polarised, split on an ideological razor edge, that the authorities come under attack. 'When nations are united in their attitudes, there is no problem for television' said Grace Wyndham Goldie. 'It is when they are divided, not only about ends but means, that television current affairs programmes must reflect this division and thereby antagonise large numbers of viewers'.[14]

This is such a time, and television cannot hope to be universally acclaimed for its impartiality and its farsightedness while the country is at odds. The authorities will have to tread warily, defend their independence of government and party when necessary, and rely on the support of public opinion in doing so. They may be helped by the fact that attacks are coming from the right and the left. To take recent examples, Mrs Thatcher's suggestion that the BBC External Services should become an instrument of propaganda seems to me a very unwise recommendation, as is the proposal made by the Publicity Committee of the Labour Party's National Executive Committee that any person speaking for the Labour Party on any television or radio programme whatsoever should be selected by the General Secretary of the Labour Party and not by the producer or by whoever wants to approach that person on behalf of a broadcasting service.

A special problem in my view arises on the industrial front where trade unions feel strongly that the broadcasters are unfair to their point of view. Industrial news seems to be immediate and superficial. We need much more exploration of the sources of industrial discontent and also much more study of what makes good management and a good company. Political and economic issues should be looked at in greater depth and over a longer time-scale. *The Money Programme* has been good at that and I'm glad that it has eventually, at least I hope so, escaped the axe of BBC economising.

The third and last aspect of television politics that I want to refer to is the accusatory interview. In a sense, the interviewer becomes the adversary. Obviously the accusatory interview has a very important place, especially if a politician is concealing a matter of public importance. It is usually more effective than a Parliamentary Question, where time for supplementaries is limited by the patience of the Speaker, and the pressure from other questioners. But the accusatory interview is not the only proper style for interviewing. Its drawback is that it seems to put the interviewee in the wrong. He is either defensive or evasive. Yet in truth he may have done nothing he should be accused of. Furthermore, accusatory interviewing is not synonymous with tough interviewing, though it's often so treated. An interviewer can be persistent, uncompromising and determined without becoming a prosecutor. He or she can also bring up fresh aspects of an interviewee, especially a public figure, by adopting a range of styles. The attitudes and opinions of politicians and other public figures should be explored in a variety of ways; the dock is not always the place in which a man or woman reveals most about himself or herself.

I turn next to violence, which is another source of unease about television. Speaking to Bernard Levin in *The Levin Interview* Robin Day referred to television's insatiable appetite for visual action and violence. It appeals, he said, to the emotions rather than the intellect. It lacks concern for the consequences of its own impact.

There has been a good deal of research into the effects of violence on television, and most of it I believe is inconclusive. There seems, if I do not misinterpret it, to be some consensus that television can affect children or young people who already show anti-social or delinquent behaviour. What we don't know is whether the sheer volume of violence on television gradually weakens and erodes our defences so that we cease to recoil when ourselves confronted with brutality and inhumanity. The Pilkington Report, in a famous passage, said that the influence of television could be 'compared with water dripping on a stone, persistent, apparently imperceptible, but in the end prevailing'. The problem is not easily resolved. Certainly broadcasters can make sure that there is no arbitrary violence simply added for kicks, and the Sims Report[15] has some trenchant things to say about that. But what about violence in the real world of Vietnam and Afghanistan, China and Cambodia, Northern Ireland and the Lebanon? It is all real, yet the world is not just about violence, war and terrorism. So in our worldwide reach for what is visually striking and sensational and urgent, the planet's mirror shows a distorted reflection. We see through a glass, darkly.

And the danger is that because we see so much that is frightful, we can begin to despair.

Again, in considering violence, we come up against people in the real world behaving as actors, or being treated as actors, the confusion of image and reality. The *Sunday Times* carried an article on 4 May 1980 which described teenage rioting at seaside resorts as being in many ways ritualistic. It's the appearance of struggle and aggression rather than the reality that the gangs seek. Now obviously this isn't entirely true. Old ladies do get mugged in alleys where there is no-one to see, and young men do get their skulls fractured in meaningless brawls. But there is evidence for the argument that violence can be turned on and off, and that it follows ritualistic patterns. Two episodes spring to my mind; one was the great Grosvenor Square demonstration in 1968, when 10,000 people marchéd upon the US Embassy to protest about the war in Vietnam. It became obvious that the confrontation between the police and the demonstrators would level out at some point, that there would be a ceiling on the escalation of mutual violence. I acquired a great deal of respect for the police on that day. At every stage where escalation seemed likely, the senior officers and the Home Office reacted with the minimum necessary to hold the situation. They did not call for mounted police when foot police would do. They did not insist on tear gas or water cannon or jeeps when mounted police could reinforce the cordons. And that day in Grosvenor Square became the epitome of how to handle a civil demonstration, an example that held up well. Because it was on the screens, it became what people expected. Television helps to create the ritual, and the ritual helps to contain the violence.

But not always. Sometimes the ritual is acted out just because television is there. We've all seen the child who makes a face at the camera. What I hadn't seen until I saw it at first hand was the demonstration to order, à la carte. This happened to me once at the old Department of Education and Science in Curzon Street. All the afternoon long, students had been circling the building, reiterating 'Short Out'[16] for hours on end. I had to go down to the ground floor to leave for a meeting. The ground floor was pulsating with students who swept past the ineffective resistance of a couple of elderly doormen. No sooner did I appear than young men in smartly striped shirtsleeves and twill trousers started shouting 'Action', followed by lights switching on and TV cameras grinding away and students thrusting their fists into the air. It was the first, but not the last time, that I have been involved in contrived demonstrations of that kind. They are, it seems to me, outside the rules, and ought to be discouraged.

All that is a litany of difficulties. So we shouldn't forget the achievement. 'The obligation', Sir Michael Swann told the Royal Television Society, 'is to serve this whole public to the best of our ability with the best programmes we can make.' Broadcasting has vastly extended people's awareness, to encompass other countries, other times, other ways of life, the arts, the sciences, the world of nature and much more. It has educated the eye and the ear of the British public so that we are no longer 'ein Land ohne Kultur und ohne Musik'. Broadcasting has raised the standards of a whole range of interests and hobbies, from dog-training to child-minding. Combined with imaginative books and journals, it has pushed out the bounds of literacy and brought higher education to tens of thousands who would never otherwise have had the opportunity. It has created aspirations outside the restrictions of income, region or social background. Ernest Bevin said shortly after the war that what was wrong with Britain was 'a poverty of aspiration'. The BBC and the broadcasters generally have done more than any other institution to enrich these aspirations and to extend our opportunities.

Broadcasting also, both radio and television, has been a great mitigator of loneliness. People live longer and more of them live alone. Radio and television act as friends, neighbours, sources of news and gossip, a surrogate village community. For the elderly unable to get about much, for the physically handicapped or for the isolated housewife, broadcasting is a lifeline. True, it can substitute for chat and talk within families and between neighbours, so that conversation dies when the set is switched on. But for many people, there would be no conversational alternative anyway.

The media hold up a mirror to the times. 'What is the mirror to reflect?' Sir Arthur fforde asked in his paper, *What is Broadcasting About?*[17] 'The best and the worst with complete indifference and without comment' he answered.

The times change. The job of Director-General, said T. C. Worsley, quoted by Hugh Carleton Greene in *The Third Floor Front*, is to detect the genuine voice of one's time, 'to spot it, foster it and give it its head'. The 1960s were challenging — bold, iconoclastic, people getting simultaneously richer and more rebellious. 'I' Imagination au pouvoir,' some excited French student wrote on the walls of the Panthéon in Paris when it looked as if Paris itself might fall. But the workers of Renault were unmoved, and the wild swinging 1960s soured into the cautious, consolidating, professional 1970s. As for the 1980s, turbulent from their inception, who can predict the 'genuine voice'? It seems to me the changes will be much more far-reaching than in the 1960s, because the orthodox political and economic thinking of both left and right will be inadequate to meet the disruption of our expectations of growth and prosperity. I think that many of our assumptions are dubious, for instance the assumption that we know how to cure inflation and how to deal with mass unemployment, given the political will. Even our faith in the progress brought by scientific discovery and technological advance is now shaken, for the world seems chaotic and unhappy as old roots are torn up and traditional communities break asunder. Internationally and nationally, the political divisions about both ends and means that Grace Wyndham Goldie feared are only too evident.

One clue to the 1980s may be found in Ralf Dahrendorf's recent book, *Life Chances*.[18] '*Life chances*,' says Dahrendorf, 'are a function of two elements, options and ligatures. Ligatures are allegiances; one might call them bonds or linkages as well.' His thesis, in a nutshell, is that options or opportunities have greatly expanded in the modern industrialised democracies. A man or woman's life chances are much less constrained by geography or background or birth or sex than they used to be even a generation ago. Options are open to us in all sorts of ways: what job we take, how long we stay in school or college, whether we move to a new town or even to a new country, whom we marry or whether we marry, whether or not we have children, how we dress, whether or not we go to church, whether we are homosexual or heterosexual. Many of these options were not open before, or were only just open, carrying with them a heavy social price. But life chances are not just made up of options. They are also made up of ligatures: relationships, friendships, communities, neighbourhoods, families, roots, remembered landscapes and buildings, the bonds of belonging to a country, a religion and a civilisation. Is it fanciful to suggest that the rupture of ligatures has made many people hate and resent change, people as different as those who moved from the old Manchester back-to-backs into the windy formless new estates on the periphery, and those dispossessed of their stony and sterile plots by the Shah's White Revolution in Iran? Everything is moving awfully fast and the landscape blurs. The old and the not-so-old find some solace in nostalgia, in the recapturing of the past they remember in films and images.

People yearn for landmarks and milestones, hence the popularity of programmes about archaeology and exotic animals, about castles and gardens and history frozen in architecture. In the riptide of change, people want something lasting to hold on to; hence, I believe, the rediscovery of communities and neighbourhoods, the many attempts to create small comprehensible worlds. On radio the long-running love affair of the public with the Archers is a prime example. In his book, *Future Shock*,[19] Alvin Toffler commented: 'Every seasoned reporter has had the experience of working on a fast-breaking story that changes its shape and meaning even before his words are put down on paper. Today, the whole world is a fast-breaking story.' Indeed: and the ambiguous adjective is chilling.

What then finally can broadcasting do in such a tumultuous world? The Annan Committee replied to the question with remarkable assurance. 'At a time when people worry that society is fragmenting, broadcasting welds it together.' I was surprised by that, because I'm not at all sure that it does. Broadcasting must reflect society's own divisions, though it may mitigate them. For example broadcasting has done a lot to mitigate divisions between the sexes, though much less to mitigate the divisions between the races. When are the BBC going to get a good black or brown news reader? We need more instances, visible ones, of what women and ethnic minorities can achieve. But while I don't see broadcasting welding society together, it does represent the context in which society operates, it does a lot to create an atmosphere and there are things it can do.

It can, as Hugh Carleton Greene advocated, focus on growth points, and make people more aware of their potential. This means showing new ways of life, patterns of living made possible by new technologies, such as micro-electronics or biotechnology, and also patterns of living based on a return to simpler life-styles. It can explore new methods of design, of goods and buildings and artefacts, that are made possible by new materials and new tools. Broadcasting can explore the future for good as well as evil. It can even help this country recover some faith in itself.

It has to analyse and test the old orthodoxies in economics and politics and explore the new — or, if I may be excused a brief excursion from impartiality, the resurrected ones, like monetarism.

Milton Friedman made splendid television, confident, impish and irrepressible. Could the much newer ideas of people like Gerald Leach in a *Low Energy Future*,[20] Fred Hirsch in *The Social Limits to Growth*[21] or Barbara Ward in *Progress for a Small Planet*[22] be expounded and questioned too? For resources are obviously strained, fossil fuels are becoming very expensive and the Third World is taking to the boats all over the world from Vietnam to Cuba, in a desperate search for a better life. This is not a blip on the radar screen, it's not a historical hiccup. It is, I suspect, a break in the projections forward, a fault-line cutting disturbingly across our assumptions that the future will be rather a lot like the past.

All that is about the options, including the ugly ones. In setting the agenda, broadcasting has to concern itself also with the other half of Dahrendorf's *Life Chances*, with the bonds and linkages. Some need to be retied; subjects that need one another have drifted apart. Science and ethics, for example. What has happened to death? Is death like birth, a matter of choice? The answer is yes, sometimes it is, and I don't mean suicide. Doctors, enthused by their new methods for keeping people alive, do not want to be disturbed by being asked if they might actually prefer to die. But radio and television should explore such questions, as television recently did in a Granada series, by bringing complementary professions together. What about art and engineering? A bridge can be beautiful; why not a factory or a machine tool? And how do we design houses adapted to the way people want to live, flexible houses, rather than adapting people to the houses?

Local radio is a marvellous link-builder. It brings together local needs and the volunteers who can meet them. It encourages local initiative; it finds jobs for teenagers and homes for abandoned children. Its potential and that of community television, is immense. One of its uses could be the creation of artificial families, bringing together the lonely old, the active retired, the over-burdened parent, the neglected child, the adolescent who needs counsel from someone other than his or her own family. The welfare state has to give up when it encounters loneliness, but radio and television do not need to do so. Phone-in and chat shows are cat's cradles of association for thousands of isolated people. There is much more, backing up broadcasts with work experience, tutorial help through colleges of further education and apprenticeship schools, and on-the-job training. In one year the BBC and the local education authorities together taught 200,000 adults to become literate and it cost very little. This need is as great, and even more immediate.

The legacy of educational broadcasting and the reputation of the Open University provide other opportunities. I was recently asked if the BBC might be persuaded to set up an Open University of Northern Europe where no one country is big enough to provide such a service for itself. Our broadcasters' experience and reputation, plus the English language are incalculable assets. We may share the English language with North America, but not our broadcasters' reputation.

I hope therefore that broadcasters will be bold in saying what they want to do and what they can do. I hope they will then tell us what it would cost and what benefits it would bring. And I hope they will then go out and campaign for it, remembering what broadcasting should be in a world beset by anarchy and war. I end by quoting Milton in *Paradise Lost* — it might be a tribute to the BBC!

> Servants of God, well done, well hast thou fought
> The better fight who singly has maintained
> Against revolted multitudes the cause
> Of truth, in word mightier than they in arms.

NOTES

1. T. Burns, *The BBC: Public Institution and Private World* (Edinburgh studies in sociology) (Macmillan, London 1977).
2. R. L. Stevenson, *Familiar Studies of Men and Books* (Heinemann, London, 1926).
3. H. G. Greene, *The Third Floor Front* (The Bodley Head, London, 1969).
4. Quoted in *The Third Floor Front*.
5. George Orwell, quoted by Arthur Koestler in *The Invisible Writing* (Hamish Hamilton, London, 1954).
6. Given to the Royal Television Society in April 1980.
7. Home office: *Report of the Committee on the Future of Broadcasting*, Chairman: Lord Annan, Cmnd. 6753 (HMSO, London, 1977).
8. That is, the administration.
9. *Report of the Committee on Broadcasting 1960*, Chairman: Sir Harry Pilkington. (Presented to Parliament June 1962.) Cmnd 1753 (HMSO, London, 1962).
10. G. Wyndham Goldie, *Facing the Nation* (The Bodley Head, London, 1977).
11. *The Carrickmore Incident*. In November 1979 it was disclosed that *Panorama*, the BBC's weekly current affairs programme, had made a film in Carrickmore,

showing some IRA terrorists apparently occupying this village in Northern Ireland. It was subsequently alleged, and denied, that the film, which was not in the event transmitted, had been made in co-operation with the terrorists.

12. *Death of a Princess*. A television film made by Antony Thomas for Associated Television, screened by ITV in April 1980. It was in the form of a dramatised documentary, piecing together the story of a Saudi Arabian princess publicly executed for adultery. The reaction of the Saudi Arabian Government was to expel the British Ambassador.

13. *The Diaries of a Cabinet Minister, vols 1–3, 1964–70* (Hamish Hamilton and Jonathan Cape, London, 1975, 1976, 1977).

14. G. Wyndham Goldie, op. cit.

15. *The Portrayal of Violence in Television Programmes: A Revised Note of Guidance*, Chairman: Miss Monica Sims (BBC, London, 1979).

16. Edward Short, then Minister of Education and Science.

17. Sir Arthur fforde, *What is Broadcasting About?* (Waterlow and Sons, London, September, 1963).

18. R. Dahrendorf, *Life Chances: Approaches to Social and Political Theory* (Weidenfeld and Nicolson, London, 1980).

19. Alvin Toffler, *Future Shock* (The Bodley Head, London, 1970).

20. G. Leach, *A Low Energy Strategy for the United Kingdom*, Science Reviews Ltd, *for* the International Institute for Environment and Development, 1979.

21. F. Hirsch, *Social Limits to Growth* (Routledge and Kegan Paul, London, 1977).

22. B. Ward, *Progress for a Small Planet* (Maurice Temple Smith, London, 1979; Penguin, 1979).

2 Asa Briggs

In this paper I want both to reflect on broadcasting and its place in society and culture and to stimulate argument. I want to reach back behind the topicalities of contemporary broadcasting to a number of fundamental issues relating to the role of authority both in broadcasting and in society and the way in which it is changing. My reflections fall naturally under four headings.

First, I want to try to explain why the members of the Preparatory Committee of this Symposium chose to start with 'authority', a concept which is not much discussed in current surveys or summaries of broadcasting problems, although it can figure in newspaper headlines and news items like 'Broadcasting system loses its authority'. Second, I want to look at the word 'authority' itself, a word, which as philosophers point out, plays a prominent part in language games. It will also be necessary under this heading to look at the current social and cultural context in which we argue about 'authority' or accept or contest it without argument, going on to place that current context in historical perspective. Third, since I believe that the concept of 'authority' is important not only in language games but in actual broadcasting activity, I want to look at the stance from which broadcasters themselves approach problems of 'authority'. Fourth and last, I want to discuss very briefly, largely by way of example, three particular facets of present broadcasting, which raise issues where 'authority', acknowledged or unacknowledged, counts as a crucial ingredient.

Why start with 'authority' and how is 'authority' related to the other themes of this Symposium?

It is conventional to distinguish between broadcasting structures and the regulatory frames which constrain them and broadcasting 'output' considered quantitatively and qualitatively. Why, however, do we need regulatory frames at all? Broadcasters are subject to 'controls' while many other communicators are not. Would not the interests of the individual be adequately met by competition between broadcasting companies? How does government view these questions—in technical or in political terms? The American language concentrates on 'regulation'. The word 'governor' is not a part of it. When and why, having delegated 'authority', does the British Government (or Parliament) fall back on its own 'authority'? How do broadcasters themselves view such questions? What other criteria do they have in mind in programming besides competitive ratings?

The reason why we chose to put 'style' second in the list of themes is because whatever else competition in broadcasting is like, it is not like competition in commodities. Questions of content, presentation, appeal and quality sometimes arise there besides questions of price. But they *always* arise when we analyse or assess broadcasting output. What, we are forced to ask, is the nature of the creative power which lies behind — even if it does not always drive — the broadcasting enterprise? When 'authority' determines or intervenes in the enterprise, how does it affect the 'style' of broadcasting? Does that 'style' reflect or influence or both?

'Authority' and 'style' may well be so closely associated that it is impossible to separate them out. Yet we can separate out different 'genres' of broadcasting — from the news bulletin to the variety show. How have the genres of broadcasting evolved and what has determined both their style and their balance within the whole broadcasting output?

We included 'choice' last because 'choice' and 'authority' are often pitted against each other and because it has often been argued — and is very frequently argued today — that listeners and viewers should be offered 'full choice'. To what extent have the present limitations on freedom of choice been set by technology? To what extent by educational and social stratification? Will the development of new technologies (i) facilitate and (ii) guarantee fuller choice as compared with choice in a period of communications scarcity? Are we moving out of an age of broadcasting into an age when communications devices of all kinds, individual and social, will be deployed in such a wide variety of ways that problems of 'authority' will disappear altogether?

All these four themes — 'authority', 'style', 'genres' and 'choice' — are interrelated. We want to explore the interrelationships in this Symposium, not to take them for granted.

My own paper can only touch upon some of the interrelationships. I approach them myself as a historian. In my history of broadcasting in this country[1] I have tried to describe how and why the power of broadcasting monopoly was broken, emphasising that the 'brute force' of chartered monopoly, which Reith extolled, carried with it an immense and pervading sense of authority. I have not talked about the consequences of the end of the monopoly, although the title of my fifth volume, if I ever write it, will perforce be 'competition'. I have already noted, however, that what happened when the monopoly was broken in England was not the advent of full commercial competition. Not only did the BBC remain in existence, but a new 'Authority'—the ITA, now the IBA—was created, the duties of which were influenced by BBC precedent. It, too, has to justify its existence, not take it for granted.

The 'authority' of the IBA was delegated to it by Parliament, whereas the BBC's authority had been delegated to it nearly thirty years before by Charter. It is an open question, however, whether the instrument of delegation made any significant difference in practice. A more interesting question is whether freedom delegated by Charter was freedom of the kind associated with models of competition (if not with imperfect competition in practice). The Charter instrument has been seized upon by more than one Director-General of the BBC as an instrument of freedom. Yet when historians contemplate the word 'Charter', beginning with Magna Carta, they do not necessarily view it like Director-Generals of the BBC. Thus, the Stationers' Royal Charter of 1557 is usually seen now as a device restricting publishing which could not outlast the subsequent multiplication of the means and products of print expansion. The Charter had to be got rid of before it was possible for print to be free. We return, therefore, to the interesting question of why, if at all, should broadcasting be treated any differently from other media of communication. The ambiguities in the word 'Charter', which start in the middle ages and are associated with fundamental arguments about 'freedoms' and 'freedom' and 'freedom' and 'privilege', come out very clearly in that deceptively simple little poem of William Blake about London which includes the memorable words 'chartered freedom'.

The nineteenth century seems to me to be a crucial century in this connection. As the economy changed and became increasingly market-dominated, the argument concerning 'communication' shifted significantly—but in England never completely—from issues of 'authority' (and patronage) to issues of 'choice' (and competition). It was then that it became a new orthodoxy that the multiplicity of outlets in print publishing represented a safeguard against the propagation and dissemination of exclusive or one-sided news and views. But the argument about freedom of communication significantly did not stop there. A new generation of critics, more concerned with underlying economic substructures in a competitive economy than with the multiplicity of outlets (which were eventually to shrink) refused to be fobbed off with too simple an approach to the logic of competition. Every single outlet, the critics argued, needed to be studied in relation to its underlying structure of ownership and the financial sources of its revenue, in particular advertising. Moreover, the 'system' as a whole needed to be scrutinised since it was clear that in practice, however many outlets there might be, there were tendencies making for standardisation rather than for diversity.

Such counter-argument had not been silenced when the BBC's monopoly was debated during the early 1950s. Against the view that monopoly was 'bad', the view could be expressed that the BBC deserved to be preserved as a monopoly because its public broadcasting was entirely 'non-commercial'. It had no owners and it was not dependent for its revenue on advertising. The more that the Press was concentrated in the hands of a few owners, the more public ownership of broadcasting needed to be preserved. Though the defenders of the monopoly lost — and they included representatives of left and right, radicals and traditionalists — the commercial forces which acquired the new competitive television companies were themselves to be 'controlled' as we have seen — on lines already laid down in relation to the BBC — by a new Authority. The major difference was that the Authority did not make programmes. The 'creative' was separated from, and placed in different hands from, those of the Authority.

It is interesting to note that it was monopoly not in sound but in television which was first breached. The special power of television was appreciated (and feared) at least as much as the special power of print had been appreciated (and feared) in the fifteenth century. Coincidentally (?) the former went with nuclear energy, the latter with gunpowder. Both new modes of communications changed all kinds of patterns of behaviour and perception which at first sight had nothing to do with communications as such. Yet the latter carried it with 'the authority of the word' as against 'the authority of the church', and the former carried it with a challenge to all formal authority. If only for this reason formal governmental (and parliamentary) authority has always tended to fear it. Parliamentary proceedings are broadcast on sound, not televised; even television party political broadcasts were slow to develop in Britain.

A few years later, as George Wedell noted,[2] there was a revealing argument about the use of the word 'authority' in relation to the Advertising Standards Authority, an Authority which derived its powers not from Parliament but from 'the industry'. 'It has always puzzled me', its Chairman, Lord Drumalbyn, said in 1962,

> why people make such heavy weather of the name 'authority'. The name is the name decided upon by the industry itself before the Authority was born. As to the 'authority' with a small 'a' it is neither more nor less than the authority which was conferred upon it by the advertising industry to be exercised over the advertising industry . . . real authority because it is voluntarily conferred and recognised by the industry. The whole basis of authority is consensus. Society is held together not by law but by respect for law and for the rules.

This interesting statement, made before there was much talk of a general 'crisis of authority', raises issues further to those already set out in this paper. Society is not just 'held together'; it changes. The nature of the dynamic (profit or propaganda, or both) is always relevant. Change from above can generate suspicion and tension; change from below conflict and confusion. In any case three sets of issues cannot be evaded. First, when we talk of 'authority' we are talking not only of individuals but of groups: in consequence, the issues posed by broadcasting are issues which cannot be sorted out simply in terms of a theory of increasing individual choice. If we leave the mass we do not return to Robinson Crusoe. Second, in any discussion of authority, 'rules' and the sanctions which sustain them must be considered along with 'law'. Those rules and sanctions can, indeed, be more binding than law itself. Third, 'consensus' is an extremely important concept. If we can speak of the consensus of an industry, what then of the consensus of a nation? If broadcasting contributes to consensus, then there is no doubt of its moral significance; if it contributes to its shattering, there is bound to be argument. What is the basis of consensus? Is it common tradition, common interest, or 'authority' plus 'deference'?

Specialists in 'communications studies' often narrow the scope of their subject till it loses contact with such bigger issues of society and culture. I hope that this Symposium will concern itself with them as Colin Cherry wished that it would do and as he was doing himself when he died. He approached such issues, of course, not as a historian but as an engineer turned philosopher. May I briefly follow him along the same lines? Before I return to the history of broadcasting, which has changed dramatically since 1962, I would like to consider briefly the word 'authority' itself and the ways in which an understanding of its history and usage can illuminate communications studies.

Authority

Authority (*Auctoritas*) is not listed in Raymond Williams's *Keywords*[3] and has no separate entry in *The Fontana Dictionary of Modern Thought*[4] (which simply states 'see under Charisma, Power'). *How should we set about analysing it?* The word is an old one with a long and complex history, religious and secular. The *Oxford Dictionary* gives amongst its meanings 'the power or right to enforce obedience, the right to command, power to influence the conduct and opinions of others, intellectual influence, title to be believed, weight of testimony, an expert in any question'.

This is a very varied list to which we would all add our own personal glosses. In my own life I have often been called upon to act upon the basis of 'authority conferred upon me'—in presenting degrees, for example, or in sending students down. I have also been referred to, not always politely, as being 'in authority' in a university or even very comprehensively as 'the authorities'. Finally I have been identified as 'an authority' on a particular period or branch of history. These are my personal glosses; Jeremy Isaacs has a different set. We are both alike, however, in that we have had 'experience of authority'. Many (most) people in society do not, whatever the income and property basis of that society, though the concept of the 'authority of the people' may give consolation or inspiration. Here then is a serious manifestation of 'them' and 'us'.

A person may be said to wield authority in two distinct senses. He may be said to be 'in authority', meaning that he occupies some office or position which entitles him to make decisions concerning how others should behave or act — either through power or influence (a significant distinction)—or he may be said to be 'an authority', meaning that his utterances are entitled to be believed. Persons in the first category include Members of Parliament, Judges, Generals, Chief Constables, Vice-Chancellors, Governors of the BBC, Members of the IBA. Persons in the second category include not only (obviously) experts (a dangerous word), but parents (though parental authority has often been challenged) and priests (though that authority has often been challenged, too, in the nineteenth and twentieth centuries as the secular debate on moral issues overlaps with but does not coincide with the religious debate).

The dividing lines between the two types of authorities are inevitably blurred. 'Those in authority over us' in England, for whom we pray in the Church of England service, include the Archbishops and Bishops of that Church. And in relation to both categories of persons there are intricate complications bound up with hierarchy (from Archbishop to priest) and status (from Professor to literary critic). The IBA has not acquired such a status.

When the concept of 'authority' is applied not to persons but to institutions, the complications increase. There may be a perceived distinction, moreover, between an 'organisation', which functions, and an 'institution' which acquires authority. The BBC became an institution very quickly. It may be claimed, indeed, that its institutionalisation can be dated from the time when its Director-General, Reith, could look the Archbishop of Canterbury in the face or even, indeed, because of his height, look down on him.

The process of institutionalisation in England is extremely interesting to trace, and it has continued into the twentieth century. I need not complicate it further by introducing the term 'Establishment' or even the term 'Academy', but I must note its relationship to 'style'. I must note, too, that when we turn in the listed dictionary meanings to words like 'power', 'influence', 'inspire' and 'title', we are further drawn towards other very complicated clusters of words like 'manipulation', 'persuasion', 'coercion', 'domination', 'hegemony'—a very broad spectrum of words—all of them studied a great deal in this century, and all of them key words in studies of media of communication.

The word 'authority' carries with it something of an aura, the kind of aura which rebels wish to dispel. William Blake—to quote him once again—talks about 'marks of authority', and there are always such 'marks' and symbols of authority as there are always rituals through which 'authority' displays itself. Max Weber's well-known distinction between traditional, charismatic and rational authority — and it is particularly useful to include the third of these — is a useful one, but all three types of authority have their aura, and the third was even more under attack during the 1960s than the first or second. As Weber himself recognised 'pure' types of authority are not to be found in the real world.

There are two other aspects of 'authority'. First, recognising 'authority' saves time. Conformity is achieved without bribes, force or discussion: X gives an order which is obeyed or expresses an opinion which is accepted. Second, all three types of 'authority' rest upon some form of consensus or to use a more useful word, perhaps, cultural coherence. De Tocqueville spoke of a 'principle' of authority. Contemporary philosophers talk of 'common frameworks' or 'rules' (threadbare talk which does not pay enough attention to 'style').

It is not merely whole societies or cultures which require some sort of coherence of this kind, but sciences and religions also, in other words those intellectual and spiritual groupings which relate 'authority' to being 'an authority'.

As soon as we start talking about coherence and authority within either context, we are forced to recognise that there are always dissenters, privileged or unprivileged, heretics and schismatics (not least in religions and sciences) and, also and not least, 'fools' and jesters, people who are 'tolerated' by 'authority' and who are often given a very definite place within a pattern of 'authority' when 'authority' is strong. We are very familiar with all these types of characters in the world of communications and I need not say much more about them. We could all produce our own list of them. We are also familiar with the view that the communications world provides the central figures, producers and performers, in a 'new Establishment' (which may begin as an 'anti-Establishment') challenging through 'charisma' (or something else) both 'rational' authority and the 'traditional Establishment'.

When during the 1960s all kinds of 'authority' were questioned and when it was frequently suggested that there were open or hidden links between different kinds of 'authority' (the 'capitalist-military-imperialist complex', for example) it was often suggested that the media were subverting 'authority'. Take, for example, the famous 1969 speech of Spiro Agnew, quoted by Anthony Smith in his extremely interesting book on television, *The Shadow in the Cave*[5] in which he 'focussed attention' on a 'little group of men' who not only enjoy 'right of instant rebuttal to every Presidential Address', but more importantly 'wield a free hand in selecting, presenting and interpreting the great issues in our nation'. 'We cannot measure their power and influence', Agnew went on, 'by the traditional democratic standards because these men create national issues overnight. They can make or break by their coverage and commentary . . . They can elevate men from obscurity to national prominence within a week. They can reward some politicians with national exposure and ignore others.'

Spiro Agnew received 80,000 letters following his speech, of which 76,000 supported the stand which he had made, and although it was Agnew, of course, not the Press or the broadcasters, who was quickly toppled from power — and the Press was to triumph at Watergate — the particular kind of attack he made has by no means entirely lost its relevance. It was, in fact, an up-to-date version, as I shall show, of an attack which was made with equal force in the eighteenth and nineteenth centuries.

The concept of 'authority', wrote Professor Richard Friedman in 1971,[6] is one of the rare ideas which has remained 'stubbornly central' both to political philosophy and to empirical social science in spite of their divergence in the twentieth century. '*Stubbornly* central' — for Friedman was writing in 1971 when the climate had made and was making the concept of 'authority' rather precarious and after an entry in the *International Encyclopaedia of the Social Sciences* of 1968 and an article called 'Reflections on Authority' in the *New American Review*, quoted by Friedman, had suggested that 'the very concept of authority has been corrupted or even lost in the modern world'.

This sense of 'corruption' or 'loss of authority' can certainly be traced back to the thirties and forties of the nineteenth century — to Kierkegaard, for example, who referred to the 'confusion' which followed after the 'concept of authority' had been 'entirely forgotten'. At a time when the Press was being held up as a 'liberating influence', dispelling ignorance and checking despotism, there were critics who considered it as both destructive of 'coherence' and debasing in its effect on standards.

The themes figure in what has often seemed to me one of the most interesting books on contemporary middle-of-the-road attitudes, Bulwer Lytton's *England and the English*, first written in the 1830s and republished in the 1870s.[7] This is what Lytton had to say about the Press around the time Kierkegaard was writing about 'confusion' and 'the end of authority'.

It is the habit of some persons more ardent than profound to lavish indiscriminate praise on the Press and to term its influence the influence of knowledge. It is rather the influence of opinion, large classes of men entertain certain views on matters of policy, trade or morals. A newspaper supports itself by addressing those classes, it brings to light all the knowledge requisite to enforce or to illustrate the views of its supporters. It embodies also the prejudice, the passion and the sectarian bigotry that belonged to one body of men engaged in active opposition to another. It is therefore the organ of opinion expressing at once the truths and the errors, the good and the bad of the prevalent opinion it represents.

This seems to me an interesting comment about the Press — and a well balanced one — if you look at the Press of Lytton's time. Yet this is only one part of his analysis. He anticipated twentieth-century writings on ratings and their influence on broadcasting when he went on to say 'That newspaper sells the best which addresses itself to the largest class, it becomes influential in proportion to its sale and thus the most popular opinion grows at last into the greatest power'. For Lytton the problem was not simply that the Press was 'making' opinion, but that by reason of seeking to get access to the largest possible market it was influencing attitudes both to 'authority' and to 'style'. If the price of newspapers were to be raised in the future, he said, they would reflect 'not mass but oligarchical sentiment'. But if, as seemed far more likely, their price were to fall, then extended circulation would give power in Britain to 'the operative'. The power of the Press, he claimed, was in general and above all else 'anti-aristocratic'.

Lytton concluded by discussing the problem of anonymity in the Press — the opposite side of the problem from personalisation in television, although they are very much two sides of the same coin. If the rules relating to anonymity of authors were relaxed, he argued, writers would be revealed as men of straw and the public would derive some benefit from 'the authority of divulged names' — this was the first time Lytton used the word 'authority' and then in a strictly limited sense. Yet looking far into the future, Lytton realised that the abandonment of anonymity would prepare the way for personalisation. 'If every able writer affixed his name to his contribution to newspapers the importance of his influence would soon attach to himself . . . he would become marked and individualised, a public man as well as a public writer, he would exalt his profession as himself '. This seems to me to be an extremely interesting forecast of the 'television personality', and if you pass from Lytton to the writings let us say of Gilbert Harding or Robin Day[8] you will find that they follow quite naturally from that kind of dynamic analysis which is there in Lytton. If 'authority' is challenged — including those 'in authority' — 'authorities' the plural of 'an authority' emerge.

Their subsequent rise is related to the growth of 'professionalisation', a favourite, if controversial, theme in recent writing on broadcasting. The expert role of the producer — even of the presenter — has been the subject of as much argument as the role of the journalist in the nineteenth century. 'Ideas about the responsibility of television are partly handed down by those who are constitutionally in ultimate control,' Robin Day wrote in 1975,[9] 'and partly thrown up from below by those like myself who are directly involved in what appears on the screen.' Those 'in ultimate control' represent devolved 'authority': those 'directly involved' represent the 'authority' of the professional. Two sorts of 'competence' are evident. Much depends on the internal structures and procedures of broadcasting organisations, but there has inevitably been tension, sometimes turning into conflict.

At this point it is interesting to note a special twist to the argument associated with the word 'authority' itself to which I must return. In Latin the word *auctoritas* is related to the modern words 'author' and 'authentic': the root is a lost verb *augere* — to augment, to increase, to enrich. An *auctor* was a man who either 'originates' — brings an object into existence — or by his efforts gives greater continuity or permanence to it. In other words there is a semantic link between 'authority' and the 'creative power' which I began by considering separately from it. God is 'the Author of all good things'. Man invents or adds to the stock.

This hidden semantic link directs our attention away from formal 'authority' and the hierarchies which sustain it to the creative role not only of the individual broadcaster but also of broadcasting itself as a human activity. Lytton appreciated such links. He followed up his chapter on the Press with a chapter on literature, a chapter on drama and a chapter on style.

He also included a fascinating passage which bears on the semantic link between the words 'authority' and 'authentic'. An 'author' is a witness adding his testimony about what he is witnessing to what is witnessed. Among the several reasons why Lytton maintained that the influence of journalism was 'anti-aristocratic' was that it not only presented facts — acting thereby as a 'witness' — but stirred argument by identifying and sharpening grievances, acting thereby as a counsel; and through this confusion of roles there was a subversion of 'authority'. Lytton believed that by 'revealing facts' the Press exerted 'a far more irresistible though less noisy sway than by insisting on theories', yet he saw it as a weakness of journalists that 'they were more influenced by each other as journalists than by the actual encounters they had with other classes' and that 'the system' struck them 'unrelieved by any affection for its component parts'.

No less a national figure than Gladstone pointed out during the course of one of the most interesting nineteenth-century debates about the moral basis of 'authority', a debate which had also drawn in John Stuart Mill, that the author as witness comes between us and 'facts' or 'ideas' and adds to them the grounds of belief in his own assurance respecting them.[10]

I have said almost as much as I have time for or dare do about the ramifications of the word 'authority'. The context in which it has been used has changed dramatically in the twentieth century — not least because of the decline of authority in religion, a subject which interested Gladstone in the nineteenth. For a robust pre-nineteenth-century opinion it is interesting to turn back to another great national figure, Dr Johnson, who warned that 'if every dreamer of innovations may propagate his projects there can be no settlement, if every murmurer at government may diffuse discontent there can be no peace, and if every sceptic in theology may teach his follies there can be no religion'. 'The remedy against these evils', he went on, 'is to punish the authors, for it is yet allowed that every society may punish though not prevent the publication of opinions which that society shall think pernicious.' There were many people in the Europe and America of the 1960s — and in many other parts of the world since — who have believed that if 'authority' is to be upheld, the 'authors' must be punished, if not prevented. There has been much discussion, too, of the distinction between those people (or institutions) holding authority *de jure* and those holding authority *de facto*.

In any such discussion, psychology and sociology point to a number of tentative conclusions concerning 'the crisis of authority' during the 1960s and 1970s. The fact that certain restraints or sanctions were removed, reduced the power of *de jure* 'authorities' and encouraged the openness of dissent. Yet as we moved into a more 'pluralistic society', where there was no general consensus on key values, there were two sets of counter-moves. New *de facto* 'authorities' emerged, often claiming greater influence than 'traditional' or 'national' authorities, while inevitably a reaction in favour of the full assertion of *de jure* authority was bound to follow. The eventual sequel is very frequently the imposing of a new authoritarian order which is far tougher in its control than the order which existed before the revolution took place.

Communications influence every stage in this process, and during the 1960s broadcasters made the most of what was significantly thought of as the 'drama' of dissent thereby giving extra influence to some of the new *de facto* authorities. It was inevitable that when a reaction in favour of 'authority' came, their own 'freedom' should be challenged.

In the *Proceedings of the Aristotelian Society* back in 1958 Professor Peters[11] made an interesting comment which I think is very relevant to the arrangement of the agenda of this conference and the identification of our themes. Given the need in broadcasting to have 'authors' who are originators, producers and witnesses, and given the fact that in public broadcasting, whether we like it or not, there are 'authorities' who 'control', even if ultimately — and often precariously — we suffer from an intellectual division of labour in considering the study of the relationship between them. Sociology and anthropology tend to deal with the first set of 'authors', when they are dealt with at all, political science with the second. Yet none of these disciplines by themselves are enough. If we are to use political philosophy to help us to sort out the notion of 'authority', as Colin Cherry wished, I suggest that in the difficult territory where sociology and political philosophy meet we cannot avoid the question as to whether the people who are the established authorities *de jure* are at the same time the *de facto* authorities. This is a crucial question about contemporary society and culture and the position of the broadcaster needs to be studied in relation to it.

What is and has been the stance of broadcasters in relation to questions of 'authority'?

In Britain we have to start with Lord Reith. We cannot get round him. He obviously had a very strong 'authoritarian' (a new word in this argument) streak, which is plain enough in his diary.[12] This streak, associated with his upbringing as well as with his personality, was important independently of his philosophy. Sir William Haley, one of his outstanding successors who shared much of his philosophy, told me once that while he thought that Reith had been a very great Director-General, nonetheless, he felt that he was a man who was always inclined to support, if not to yield, to authority. He, William Haley, by contrast, he went on, was a man who started with a strong identification with dissent. This was partly because he had been brought up in the newspaper world, partly because he had been born in the Channel Islands and had worked in Manchester, a centre of liberal dissent.

Whatever the differences of personality and upbringing, when we look back from our present vantage point it is not so much the differences between Reith and Haley which stand out as their similarities. Both of them lived in a period when news was not dealt with by the broadcasting authorities in the same way as it was dealt with in the Press; it arrived mainly via the agencies and was presented in a straight objective manner in the form of 'bulletins'. Both believed that broadcasting had long-term objectives which transcended the rhythms of the day and the topicalities of current news issues. Both were very suspicious of television, not on the grounds that it might subvert authority, but that it trivialised and distorted, in other words that it was not sufficiently 'authoritative' (a significantly different adjective from 'authoritarian').

It is very interesting to note that in *Broadcast Over Britain*,[13] a book which I must have read a hundred times, and in which I always find something new whenever I reread it, Reith does not use the word authority once; I believe, indeed, that he took it completely for granted. Whenever he uses the word 'authorities', which he does once or twice, he is talking about 'authorities' in the second sense of the word authority that I mentioned, as the plural of 'an authority'. 'We have set out to secure', he writes, 'and have succeeded in securing the co-operation and advice of recognised authorities and experts in all branches of our work.' He believed that the role of the broadcasting medium was to give more people access to that kind of 'authoritative' influence which had hitherto been available only for the few. 'It is true', he said,

> that the appeal of the ear may not be quite as quick as that of the eye, but a wireless is concentrated essence, it is also direct, so that each listener may feel that he is being personally addressed. The keen interest in broadcasting is due in large measure to the essential directness of the service in whatever line it may be. Till the advent of this universal and extraordinarily cheap medium of communication a very large proportion of the people were shut off from first hand knowledge of the events which make history. They did not share in the interests and diversions of those with fortune's twin gifts — leisure and money. They could not gain access to the great men of the day, and these men could deliver their messages to a limited number only. Today all this has changed.

That was Reith's grand conception of the significance of broadcasting in the twentieth century as a new force; it was to recruit an audience, not service a market. 'Authority' was necessary not just on technical grounds but on grounds of values. The origins of public broadcasting, managed not by chartered corporation but by business company, distinguish it completely from the set up of the print medium. A further term which we should bring into the discussion of 'authority', therefore, is 'public interest', an equally difficult term, elusive and ambiguous. It is a term which we would have to look at in detail if we wanted to make much progress in justifying the theory and practice of limited 'regulation' of broadcasting in the United States; and it is an equally important term to analyse if we examine in detail the post-Reithian history of the BBC.

I said that it is very difficult to get away from Reith in discussing the British approach to 'authority'. He even figured in the recent debate on *Death of a Princess* in the House of Lords. When Lord Carrington was asked what Lord Reith would have done if he had been faced with the problem of whether *Death of a Princess* should be broadcast or not, he immediately gave the only proper reply — that it was very difficult to imagine Reith as Chairman of a commercial television company. I think I can just imagine him, although I am sure that if he had been he would still have been inspired by a very strong sense of public interest. It was that which counted for him, not the actual method of financing public broadcasting.

Of course, the identification of that public interest is far more difficult in peacetime than in wartime and in the 1960s, 1970s and 1980s than in the 1940s and 1950s, and I drew attention rightly, I believe, in *Governing the BBC*,[14] to a letter from Sir Ian Jacob, a later Director-General of the BBC (and the Director-General who had to face up to competition) in which he said in 1978 that governing the BBC in the 1970s was a far more difficult job than governing the BBC had been in his time.

There were at least seven reasons for this and broadcasting inside and outside the BBC had to take account of all of them: (i) public opinion, at the same time more vocal and more divided; (ii) more assertive pressure groups, a term not used during the 1920s; (iii) professionalisation with its own set of values; (iv) an erosion of confidence in all 'authority'; (v) unionisation with its own set of interests, a 'countervailing power' with an authority (and symbols of authority) of its own; (vi) governmental uneasiness about the difficulty of governing which could even lead to complaints being made that broadcasting could not govern itself by people who were incapable of governing the country (however attractive at the time theories of 'hiving off' might be, there was always an unwillingness to trust intermediate institutions); and (vii) parliamentary un-willingness to back government wholeheartedly. Broadcasting issues became political issues, partly because one 'side' in politics — the Labour side — had less influence over the media than the other side and was uneasy about control, access and contact, partly because 'media philosophies' advanced by (some) socialists seemed to threaten 'freedom' as it had been passed on from generation to generation.

I tried to show in *Governing the BBC* (which might have been, perhaps should have been, accompanied by a parallel volume on the IBA) how the stances of those 'in authority' in broadcasting depend on their origins, background, education and experience. They do not operate in a void. I tried to show just how important (and increasingly important) the position of 'Chairman' is. We know very little of how and why the Chairmen are appointed (except in retrospect through autobiography). Parliament is not consulted, and there is obviously an element of patronage which counts for at least as much as knowledge or general suitability. If we are to check cynicism it is of the utmost importance, at least for the concerned public, to know who are the people involved in the overall direction and guidance of the broadcasting enterprise. Merely 'being there' will not provide them with adequate authority. Nor can (or should) their claim to public authority rest entirely on acceptability to the political party in power.

The fact that there is no great competition for the 'in authority' posts suggests not only that there is doubt about the relationship with the government (licence fee, levy, etc.) but that there is uneasiness about the internal relationships in broadcasting between 'authority' and *'auctores'* — authority in this case including managerial as well as constitutional authority. It has been fashionable to associate problems with one side only — the 'intervening' authorities who can be blamed for all failures to understand the 'processes of creation' in broadcasting. Yet this is one-sided. Years ago, before television won the first great battle over sound, John Wain rightly insisted that it is necessary

> to take a sceptical attitude towards the professionalism that makes the television medium have a mystic value in itself. Television producers are understandably anxious to put a high technical gloss on their work to produce beautifully finished programmes that use the possibilities of the medium to the full. But this anxiety can grow into a tyranny. If television is determined, as it seems to be, to challenge radio on its own ground, to become the mass medium that handles everything, then it will have to learn not to insist on re-making everything in its own image. It will have to cultivate the cheerful ostrich-like digestion of radio. Only the other day I heard a serious discussion brought on in the education service as 'just not television'. What is this television that has this lofty power of imposing its own nature on every kind of material?[15]

The importance of the question has not diminished, although by now questions of the relative cost of producing certain kinds of television programmes have become more relevant to the debate about what different media can and should do than argument about their inherent characteristics. It should be added that in both sound and television 'creative' broadcasting suffers if everything is left to the full-time 'professionals'. Commissioning is as necessary an element in the creative process of broadcasting as devolution is in its management.

Facets of broadcasting where 'authority' counts as a crucial ingredient

In seeking to identify particular facets of broadcasting where 'authority' is a relevant issue we find ourselves entering territory where there is often a difference of stance between broadcasters and 'authorities' — with the name of the public being invoked even when the public itself is relatively indifferent. The number of issues has certainly increased, as Lord Annan pointed out in relation both to 'news' and documentary programmes (where the author is witness) and 'entertainment' (where the author is creator). 'For years British broadcasting had been able successfully to create, without alienating government or the public, interesting and exciting popular network programmes from the world of reality as well as the world of fantasy', the Annan Committee reported in 1977. 'These now began to stir up resentment and hostility, and protests against their political and social overtones.'

Three facets I would choose myself — and different people would doubtless choose others — are (i) confusing still further the already confused boundaries between the world of reality and the world of fantasy, 'fact' and 'fiction'; (ii) concentrating on topicalities (including tomorrow's events) to such an extent that perspective is lost; and (iii) choosing 'styles' of presentation proclaimed to be 'popular' without necessarily being so, styles which are calculated to destroy both the 'authentic' and the 'authoritative'. (Language itself is closely involved along with style at this point, and there is a sharp contrast between the language and style of domestic and external services of the BBC which deserves to be studied in this symposium.)

There have long been complaints about the blurring of 'fact' and 'fiction', but television (with its huge audience) is particularly effective as a 'blurrer'. One of the most interesting brief articles I have read on such blurring appeared in the United States *TV Guide* in 1976 — 'Fact or Fiction — Television Docudramas' by Bill Davidson, who himself had had experience of writing 'lies' — he uses the word himself. He points particularly to the moral problems of writer and producer — distorting facts to make a better story — but notes too that there is misrepresentation. The 'author' can be corrupted: the sense of the 'authentic' is lost. Of course, because of the choice of themes, the chemistry need not seem dangerous: the greatest dangers arise when 'fact' and 'fiction' are blurred in international themes where the public may be ill-informed or misinformed to start with — some of these involve issues of peace and war — or in national themes where 'objectivity' and 'clarity' particularly count.

I believe that it is the duty of 'authority' *within the broadcasting system* to monitor programmes which blur, although it is obviously preferable if writers and producers can take account of the perils of such blurring at a far earlier stage. I recognise that there are — and have been through time — many different kinds of imaginative fusions of 'fact' and 'fiction' and that the 'author' may be driven to present 'art' to his public in this form, but I do not regard every intervention in this field — and there are interventions which stop short of 'censorship' — by 'public broadcasting authority' to be a threat to the 'freedom' of the author. The television audience is a different kind of audience from the more selective audiences individual authors seek to reach. What seems to me crucial in the evaluation of intervention (itself a necessary task for critics and historians) is the exploration of the element of deceit in the fact/fiction and the likely consequences of deliberate misrepresentation. There may well be a healthy difference between the attitude of 'public broadcasting authority' and the government, but unless 'public broadcasting authority' recognises its own responsibilities, there will always be pressure, potentially dangerous pressure, for government itself to intervene.

The second facet — concentrating on topicalities (including tomorrow's events) to such an extent that perspective is lost — is a consequence of the 'news revolution' which has influenced the patterns of post-Reithian daily broadcasting (and has itself been influenced by new technologies) far more than any other force. The fact that so many people with a 'news background' have risen to prominence in broadcasting has changed the balance. It has also led to a shift in broadcasting costs which adds rigidity to all broadcasting budgets and makes more difficult all discussions about 'cuts'. The need for 'competition' on the same terms between Press and broadcasting agencies is too easily taken for granted within public broadcasting (just as is competition in all matters between BBC and IBA); and when the range of possible ways of handling news differently is discussed by people outside public broadcasting there is an immediate defensive reaction of the kind that critics of public broadcasting of all shades most resent. The 'authority' of BBC or

ITN in its news presentation rests on the 'authenticity' of its witness; and because 'authenticity' may depend on very direct witness the pre-war reliance on news agencies (strongly supported, as it was, by the Press) was obviously restrictive. The 'immediacy' of television is one of its characteristics which should not be left untapped. Yet there is rightly continuing uneasiness about the influence of present news policies on societies and cultures, particularly when tomorrow's news is anticipated and yesterday's news is forgotten. The long-term rhythms of life are distorted, the more profound (and structural) issues of a society left relatively unexplored.

The great change can be illustrated through the collapse of *genres* (e.g. 'the talk') or the rise and fall of satire, each a subject worth a symposium in itself, and transformations of style both through idiom and presentation. Take this comment on the announcer in the *Radio Times* for July 1929:

the style of the broadcast announcer is, of all styles, the most impersonal, severe and correct. It is designed to communicate facts and not to express shades of opinion or interpret emotions. It is far too 'icily regular, splendidly dull' to satisfy either the average listener or speaker, and it is not likely universally to be emulated. But as a background to other, and more 'human' styles, it is good.

We are on a different planet. The implications (for news readers as well as announcers) should be part of the agenda of this symposium: they constitute the third facet — out of many possible facets — which I chose as examples.

I have three final reflections. First, in suggesting that we examine 'authority' I am not pleading for 'safe' broadcasting. I am urging us to disentangle issues which touch on both the creativity and responsibility of public broadcasting. The word 'accounting' which is so often used seems to me as narrow and superficial as the word 'regulation'. Second, although for reasons of time I have dealt mainly with British experience, I hope that we can pass on in this symposium, which is an international symposium, outside, to the international frame. It is necessary to remember that the world at present is not operating on norms and standards which have been derived through the particular chronological sequences or structural complexities of European social and cultural history. If we are to understand comparative broadcasting (or, for that matter, external services broadcasting, and broadcasting by foreigners back to their own countries) we have got to understand comparative approaches to 'authority'. It will be necessary to bring anthropologists as well as historians into the study, and that is why I am glad that there are anthropologists present. I do not believe that there is one single model which will enable us to understand the way in which broadcasting raises questions of 'authority', particularly the model of this country which in many ways is unique.

Third, I want to place on the agenda once more the relationship between 'authority' and 'choice'. There is no guarantee that the development of new technologies making possible greater individual choice will either maximise that choice by offering the widest range of alternatives, paying attention to quality as well as to quantity, or that individuals will be either willing or able to make the fullest use of whatever choice is made available to them. The most ambitious development of communications devices in a society and culture without the development of education will not offer an adequate answer to social and cultural deprivation. Nor, indeed, it is fair to add, will the development by itself of an educational system geared to schooling. If public broadcasting agencies relegate their own 'educational role' to a low place on their agendas, they forfeit part of their claim to be public. As for the role of the market itself in social and cultural matters, the most cogent account of its limitations is still in my view that offered in the Pilkington Report.

I do not believe that however sophisticated new technologies become, they will eliminate either the book or 'broadcasting' as a community activity, including a national community activity. There are many occasions when we share rather than choose as individuals. Societies and cultures are richer rather than poorer when there is a broad range of such occasions — not only news occasions or 'media events' but occasions for laughter (we still share much of our humour across class lines) and tears. And as soon as we begin to talk of such sharing we cannot evade issues of 'authority' and 'style'.

NOTES

1. A. Briggs, *The History of Broadcasting in the United Kingdom*, vols I–IV (Oxford University Press, 1961–1979).

2. E. G. Wedell, *Broadcasting and Public Policy* (1968).
3. R. Williams, *Keywords: A Vocabulary of Culture and Society* (Fontana, London, 1976).
4. *The Fontana Dictionary of Modern Thought*, eds Alan Bullock and Oliver Stallybrass (Collins, London, 1977).
5. A. Smith, *The Shadow in the Cave: a study of the relationship between the broadcaster, his audience and the state* (Allen and Unwin, London, 1973).
6. R. B. Friedman, 'On the Concept of Authority in Political Philosophy', in *Concepts in Social and Political Philosophy*, R. E. Flathman (ed) (Collier-Macmillan, 1973).
7. Edward Bulwer-Lytton, *England and the English*, 2 vols (Bentley, London, 1933).
8. For example, Gilbert Harding, *Along my Line* (Putnam, London, 1953) and *Master of None* (Putnam, London, 1958).
9. R. Day, *The Case for Televising Parliament* (Hansard Society for Parliamentary Government, 1964) and *Day by Day: A Dose of my own Hemlock* (William Kimber, London, 1975).
10. W. E. Gladstone, 'On the Influence of Authority in Matters of Opinion', *Nineteenth Century*, 1877.
11. R. S. Peters, 'Authority', *Proceedings of the Aristotelian Society*, 32, 1958.
12. *The Reith Diaries*, ed. Charles Stuart (Collins, London, 1975).
13. J. Reith, *Broadcast over Britain* (Hodder and Stoughton, London, 1924).
14. A. Briggs, *Governing the BBC* (British Broadcasting Corporation, London, 1979).
15. John Wain, *The Listener*, July 1965.

3 Jeremy Isaacs

'In the end someone has to have the responsibility for decid-
ing . . . what can be broadcast in particular circumstances at any
given time. In our view, the ultimate responsibility should rest with
the Authorities . . . '

Annan Committee, Report on the
Future of Broadcasting

To claim authority, one must exercise it. No-one I have encountered in a working life spent in television exercised it more
willingly than my first boss, Sidney L. Bernstein. Now ennobled,
Bernstein was known then to the staff at Granada as Mr Sidney,
distinguishing him from his able but less flamboyant brother Mr
Cecil, or, more directly and succinctly, as SLB. Sidney Bernstein
was then, this was 1958, I think Chairman and Joint Managing
Director of Granada Television. Titles, offices, chains of executive
command were irrelevances. He ran the company. Authority was
vested in one man, and we knew it.

SLB approved plans for building, lettering for notepaper, menus
for the canteen. SLB corrected the text of advertising copy and of
newspaper press releases. SLB altered the punctuation of scripts.
SLB suggested subjects for programmes, directors for drama,
presenters for public affairs. SLB telephoned after transmission with
his criticisms, led discussions with his questions, ended them with his
verdict. SLB inspected lifts, corridors, kitchens, lavatories for
cleanliness; office desks for tidiness; wastepaper baskets for waste.
On every office wall there hung, by his decree, a portrait of Phineas
T. Barnum, reminding each one of us that this was show-business.
The face that watched us as we worked was Barnum's but the
presence was Bernstein's alone, and the inspiration.

Granada began broadcasting with a tribute to the BBC and for a
decade saw itself as providing the leaven in the ITV lump. No
matter that its programmes cannily included *Criss Cross Quiz*,
Coronation Street, *The Army Game*, it was to more rarefied programmes
that the Bernstein flair for publicity tirelessly drew attention; the

plays of Arthur Miller, documentaries on 'difficult' subjects; current affairs programmes that crusaded for betterment and change, anyway on a carefully selected list of topics. Granada, at Rochdale in 1958, was first to cover a by-election by discussion among the candidates; Granada would have cameras as of right at election counts and in party conferences, and would leave no string unpulled to get them there. Granada broadcast with a purpose, aiming to provide the best of every type of programme, the best as one man conceived it.

Sidney Bernstein was a hard man to work for. Arguing the detail of every script for so modest a programme as *What the Papers Say*, a weekly review of the Press, was a wearing business for a tyro producer. But Bernstein's yea was yea and his nay was nay. (The problems began when his mind was not made up, and nothing went ahead until it was.)

Every Thursday afternoon I read the script of *What the Papers Say* over the telephone from Manchester to the company's lawyers at the Bouverie Street firm of Goodman, Derrick, and on critical occasions to Arnold Goodman himself. (This was peculiarly necessary since Bernstein was usually involved in litigation with at least one newspaper group, most often Beaverbrook.)

'You may publish that', Goodman would say. Or sometimes: 'No. You may not publish that. I advise against it'. Or sometimes: 'You may if you wish publish that but there are risks attached to doing so. The decision must be Mr Bernstein's'. 'How great are the risks?' 'Perhaps a one in three chance of an action for libel against you, and a one in four chance of its succeeding.' 'Thank you, I shall let Mr Bernstein know your view.' On occasion, we published. A responsible proprietor decided whether or not to broadcast, subject, as we all are, to the law of the land, and accountable to a public regulatory body, the Independent Television Authority, grand but remote.

It was a strange introduction to broadcasting to work for a company large enough to aspire to all-round excellence, national prominence, international reputation, yet small enough to be dominated by one man. And those were pioneering days. The company was new; most of us were beginners, everything was done for the first time. Mistakes were legion, but there was excitement in the air. We knew what we were saying, and why we were saying it, what we thought of what we'd said yesterday, and why we'd say it differently tomorrow. And we knew soon enough what *he* thought of what we'd done. And, on a rare occasion, we told him to his face what we thought of what he was doing. I sometimes think that the early days of Bernstein's Granada may have been not unlike the early days of Reith's BBC.

'Who do you think should run the BBC?' Bernstein asked me one day, standing on the tarmac at Manchester Airport. It was 1960, and a new Director-General was to be appointed to succeed Sir Ian Jacob. I muttered the name of some distinguished public servant, noted as much for tact and diplomacy as for his ordered mind. It was the wrong answer. 'Not the right sort of man at all', said Sidney Bernstein.

I was glad enough to leave Granada. But I never found its like again. Television programmes have been run that way. Not television companies. And, as ITV settled down, the Independent Television Authority began to claim a share in the editorial process. The Director-General, Sir Robert Fraser, was concerned that Granada's current affairs programmes were too opinionated, or rather that they were opinionated at all, when the 1954 Television Act specifically forbade that any programme should express any view of its own in any matter of current political or industrial controversy. 'Every single programme', Sir Robert complained, accurately enough, of a series called *Searchlight*, 'directly contravened the Television Act, with the possible exception of a programme on cruelty to children. And even there', he added, 'I am not sure you should not have included someone saying that cruelty to children was a good thing.' When I and others argued to Sidney Bernstein that this was nonsense and that in *What the Papers Say*, for instance, presented by a rotating trio of differing political outlook, the programme should reflect not just what the papers said, but what the presenter thought both of them and of the issues they wrote about, he could not accede. 'I agree with you', he would reply. 'But I cannot allow it. The Act forbids it, and I have pledged my word, in a signed contract, to operate this franchise under the Act.'

There was no answer to that, except to change the Act. In the end it did change, allowing programmes to express opinions, if properly balanced over a series as a whole. But the mild enlargement of journalistic freedom was matched over the years by a marked strengthening of the Authority's (soon the Independent Broadcasting Authority's) watchfulness over the television companies, and by a willingness on the IBA's part to shift the ultimate decision as to what may or may not be broadcast away from the owners, bosses, directors, editors, programme producers in the several television companies to one central point of responsibility, the Authority itself, to its officers, to the Chairman or even, in the last resort, to the Chairman and Members sitting as a body appointed under statute to supervise commercial broadcasting in the United Kingdom.

This process was hastened and reinforced when, in 1969, a private citizen appealed to the courts to stop the broadcasting of an ATV documentary on Andy Warhol which, it was claimed, would offend against public decency. The court ruled that the relevant statutory body, the Independent Broadcasting Authority, should fulfil its duties under the Act and decide whether the programme might be broadcast. Lord Denning stressed that to that end the Chairman and Members should view the programme themselves. They did. The programme was shown, and made little impact. The court decision had a lasting effect. The then Chairman, Lord Aylestone, acknowledged his responsibilities in a telling homely phrase: 'It is right that he who has to carry the can should feel the whole weight of it'.

The Annan Committee on the Future of Broadcasting came firmly to the conclusion that it was right that the Authority — in ITV the IBA, in the BBC the Board of Governors—should carry the can. By their verdict they reinforced that rule and practice. Yet that same careful consideration led them also to descry the nonsense that follows if all-important editorial decisions in expanded broadcasting services — both BBC and IBA subsume simultaneously several voices — are taken at one central point. Annan counselled the Independent Broadcasting Authority against detailed intervention in editorial decisions, and recommended they should intervene less frequently.

It is natural for students of broadcasting, and for commentators on public affairs, to concern themselves most in broadcasting matters with the question of ultimate authority in the decision process, and with relations between broadcasting authorities and government when decisions are thought to touch on the national interest. But it is natural for the broadcaster to begin much further back.

Where broadcasting systems are merely mechanisms of social control, there is no ambiguity about where power lies. In totalitarian societies the programme controller is literally the programme controller. He answers to the state.

Where broadcasting is a function of the market, merely a

mechanism for maximising revenue from advertisements maximising the volume sale of goods, a similar simplicity obtains. The initiation, development, launch, retention of a programme in the schedules depends on no individual's judgment of its worth, but only on a dispassionate, mathematical calculation of its reach, percentage point, to an audience similarly reduced to statistics.

In each such society, of either mould, broadcasting systems can be constructed as perfect models to fulfil clear, chosen ends. In neither, once power is apportioned and control systems established, is there need for discussion or argument as to where authority lies. Functionaries do not argue, they function.

In the Soviet Union broadcasting serves the state, no less in its relations with other countries than internally. Western broadcasters may be made chillingly aware of this when attempting to make programmes there to be seen here. Contracts permitting filming normally begin with clauses affirming that the object of the transaction is 'to foster friendly relations between our two countries'. After that, offend who dare.

Once, party to such a misguided attempt, I offended deeply, by sending with the film unit a researcher who spoke fluent Russian. The bureaucracy slipped. The visa was granted. The researcher was able to speak freely to ordinary citizens of Moscow without the intervention of the interpreter and guide assigned to us by Moscow Television. On a flying visit, I was asked to send him home. I refused. The researcher, a wild sort of man, then involved himself and another in a motor accident. Both suffered minor injuries. Again, I was summoned. 'And now', said my Soviet counterpart, 'we will have a "corrida" and we will try your man and we will sentence him to death. He will be executed, unless, of course, he commits suicide first.' He smiled. It was only a joke. The chill, however, lingered on his lips.

What was serious and systematic was the attempt to control what was shown to us, said to us, shown by us, said by us. In this case, two defiant harbingers of dissent faced our camera. The film was smuggled out of Russia and eventually, at the cost of a painful breach in Anglo-Soviet friendly relations, broadcast. Authority in Soviet broadcasting rules by fear.

No difficulty attaches to reporting freely from the United States. No need to smuggle out film. But it is at least as hard, if not harder, to make for American networks the programmes that do not fit the system's requirements. I do not mean that American programme makers do not like to make the programmes they do make. Some of them do. But whoever works on those production lines accepts in doing so the standard specifications governing what is produced on them. After months of research, planning, shaping, refining the prototype, it is tested in the market. If it fails it is discarded, or redesigned. If it succeeds, production begins. The factory takes on a work force. Writers, producers, directors, actors, technicians assemble to make a product, cranking up to meet delivery dates at time-and-motion studied speed. If the programmes fail to reach market targets, the production line halts. If they succeed, the line speeds up. Miraculously some goods of genuine quality survive this process. But the system is not planned for miracles.

The network functionaries who commission what the factories produce plan to minimise risk. What has not been market pretested, research-approved, positively-piloted, formula-moulded, precision-machined is not, dare not even be contemplated for transmission. No possible gain could ever match the certain penalty for failure. Why take the risk? The executives who programme for US network television are intelligent men. Their minds are somewhat scarred, however, by self-inflicted lobotomies. On television, they have no opinions. Or no opinions on which they dare act. 'I like the programme', one is told, if one offers a play or documentary made in Britain to a different formula, or no formula at all. 'But it is too good for us.' Authority is the market.

And authority is the network clearance officer. 'No writer, no director, no producer, no head of drama, no director of programmes, no managing director, no chairman, no official of the regulatory body decides what is broadcast,' I was told in one office. 'The network clearance executive in this office is a retired military officer. He has it in his contract that no-one, not even the network president, may query his decision.'

For the functionary no argument, because no problem. The quiet of those carpeted corridors is a silence which gives consent to forces which it is professional death to question. It is characteristic of capitalist and communist broadcasting systems alike, at least in their purest forms, that the power of ultimate decision is outside, in the politburo, or in the market. Policies, therefore, are laid down, decisions handed down, from the top. It is for those below to fulfil requirements they have had no part in formulating. They have no authority, except to pass on to those below them the wishes of their masters.

'I asked you for a pound of apples. You have brought me a pound of pears. Take them back and bring me a pound of apples.' Thus the erstwhile programme controller of a major ITV company in days of yore. His utterance obtained a modest notoriety. It deserved wider circulation. For it reaffirmed in British television a practice of unrestrained commercialism, though a commercialism sheltered from the harsh winds of competition. And the thrust was the same, from the top down.

But the essence of the television which a responsible democracy exhibits, which we ought to cherish, and which I seek to recommend, is that for much of the time, first decisions are as important as last decisions. In the beginning is the idea. And the particular idea is very seldom from the top of the broadcasting organisations down but from the creator inside up, or from the creator outside in, from the writer who has something to say and a way of saying it that suggests television as a medium to be used. And writers are an anti-authoritarian crowd. All television consumes quantities of material, demands volume production. All television depends on production lines. But, for any television service that seeks to challenge its audiences and renew its own energies, it is essential that somewhere in the factory, or better, perhaps, completely outside it, there are men and women at work, challenging current orthodoxies, pushing new ideas, reaching for new forms. Without them, whether dramatists, film-makers, comedians, journalists, television cannot hope to do other than reproduce tomorrow the formulae of today.

It is argued, by those who seek drastically to change society, that that is precisely what it does; that broadcasting in the United Kingdom, reproducing the views of a narrow consensus, is no more than an instrument for maintaining the status quo. This charge depends in part upon ignoring the work that radical writers do for television — Jim Allen, Trevor Griffiths, Barry Keefe, G. F. Newman, Dennis Potter are but a few of those whose plays could not possibly have been broadcast in the UK if conformity were all. But the charge is a serious one, at least as serious as the complaint that the medium is subversive of all that most people hold most dear.

It is not obligatory on broadcasting institutions to accommodate the first work of every graduate of film school or luminary of the fringe. But it is essential, in a plural society, for broadcasting institutions to welcome the work of the best of that society's critics, above all of those who speak through their art. If gifted writers and directors find television too conformist to want to work for it, then it is time for broadcasters to examine their schedules, and widen, if they can, the range of voices that are heard. Certainly, television drama in the UK has become in recent years too comfortably concerned with the past, and needs again to be more involved in the uncertain present. Broadcasting in plural democracies will always attract the fire of those who seek change in society, as of those who wish to shore it up. Broadcasting institutions are at the heart of these disputes. Broadcasting authorities are bound to reconcile the creative impulse to utter, art and argument, with a decent respect for the susceptibilities of society as a whole; a common concern for what divides us with a common interest in what we share. Whatever decisions they take, ban or publish, they cannot win. But someone must decide.

Is there in fact, though, a balance to be kept between any one programme, however fierce, uncompromising, excoriating, and the interest of society as a whole? In a monolith state certainly. Every drop of water helps erode the stone. But, in a plural society, we can live, can we not, with the suggestion that Borstal[1] is repressive, or that some policemen (like some of the rest of us) are corrupt, or that sexuality has many facets, or that the devil, in a writer's Christian gaze, will appear in new disguise? The systematic claim that society is rotten through and through needs to be argued not asserted; assertion of it needs to be questioned, argument to be answered. A national broadcasting system would betray its trust if it propagated such argument without reply. But the individual voice of dissent speaks not just against society but for society, for something in that society which others may recognise also. For society is a babble of voices, a clash of interests, a sum of sects. Every powerful utterance offends, every new idea startles. Broadcasting must utter and broadcasting Authorities, in weighing the consequence of uttering, need not poise the scrawny pipe of one poor programme against the city walls of centuries. Not even for the trumpet will the walls fall, unless the foundations are, indeed, rotten.

Whatever the argument for freedom unrestrained, it will not happen. You cannot legislate for total licence, unless you legislate for anarchy. Liberty has always some limit. And in broadcasting, in the UK at any rate, the limit on outlets has imposed restraints, and is likely to continue to do so. More will want to be heard than will ever get on the air. So what authority, and where, and whose?

Authority, first of all, is to be dispersed, delegated; to be exercised at different levels, allowed, in due measure, to many. Not absolute authority, of course. In the last resort that will lie with those statutorily enjoined to exercise it, and behind them with Parliament.

Those who speak and write with authority should do so freely also on television. The author of a play or of a documentary who has suggested a theme, wrestled with shaping it, writing it, filming it, polishing and editing it, has authority that commands respect. Else why commission him? Why fund his work? He is not lightly to be told, this shall not pass.

The reporter has authority. He is not there to tell us how he would reshape the world. If he does, he will not be there for long. But if he writes from Africa, because he knows Africa, or from Arabia, or from Cambodia, he should have his say, his judgement informing his pictures. It is not for his superiors to rewrite his text at their desks. If he is not trusted, he should not have been sent. Once sent and returned, let him utter.

The producer, too, of regular current affairs programmes and of news has authority. He must have it. He cannot work without it. He must decide among all the options open to him where to commit resources, when to send a crew, what reporter to assign, when to transmit. When he decides, action follows. Without his decisions no programme. (The editor's indecision is final.) Remove his authority, and he cannot act.

Above him, though here responsibilities are less clear, a head of department, above him a channel controller, a director of programmes, has each his or her sphere. The head of department, talking to the producer, watching his work, has to see what else is needed to complement or contrast what one programme can show. A channel controller will probably want to feel that all human life is there. If he controls more than one channel, certainly so.

The hierarchy functions. Yet in crisis, when confronted with really difficult decisions, the structure may not take the strain. A writer writes, commissioned by a producer; the head of department approves; the play is made. The channel controller refuses to transmit it. Outcry. And understandably. What has happened is a betrayal of trust. It is easy for the busy executive, taking a long view, to feel that a necessary editorial decision, within a clearly delimited area of responsibility, has had to be taken, has been taken and there is an end of the matter. But it never is. Cancelling a play is not cancelling an order for paper. Too much pain is involved.

Hard decisions have to be taken, shoddy work should not be screened, libels not perpetrated, gross *bêtises* not committed. Second thoughts *are* sometimes best. All the same, an editorial decision not to broadcast what others' earlier editorial decisions have commissioned, revised, started, completed must call into question the worth of the chain of editorial command and the judgement of key figures in it.

Referring upwards through the hierarchy is not the answer unless at every level there is a shared, articulate belief in broadcasting's point and purpose, against which background particular judgements are made and decisions taken. And the more layers in the hierarchical structure, the more the chance of disagreement and wobble on the way. 'Should we do the economy or Europe on Monday?' is a question that *Panorama's* editor may properly discuss with the Head of Current Affairs. 'Should we commission three plays from Edward Bond?' is a question the channel controller must face up to at the outset. The producer who suggests the commission therefore, if he is to be able to deal with the author with authority, must himself face the controller at that outset and be authorised to proceed by him. Should that controller refuse, or agree and change his mind, he must give reasons to the producer and, once the work is begun, to the writer also. To do so is to show proper respect for the authority of others, now overruled.

Authority then, within the structure of broadcasting organisations as we know them, is best exercised as leadership towards a common purpose, best based on shared experience. Authority is best exercised not remotely and from on high, but at close enough quarters for one to know the other, sense the mood, read the mind. Authority must explain itself. Discussion should precede decision, reason follow it, else all is arbitrary, brittle, insecure. Authority is to be delegated, proximate, accountable; clear, near, open.

The man at the top, assisted if he chooses by the collective wisdom of colleagues, ought to decide what will or will not be broadcast by them. He will have powers equivalent to those of a newspaper editor, answerable to a proprietor, subject to the law, accountable in the long term for his general conduct of affairs to the appropriate external regulatory body.

He will, on occasion, have to decide whether or not to publish matter that may give great offence, may be thought to harm a national interest. *Death of a Princess* reminds us that such decisions are not hypothetical but real. The editor may well keep the supervisory body informed of what he is doing, but his decision it ought to be. In the case of ATV's *Death of a Princess*, the IBA, although fully informed, did not intervene. No-one, I think, foresaw quite the clamour and the consequences for British trade that followed that decision to broadcast. Even if they had, the decision might well have been exactly the same. That decisions to publish have consequences that governments themselves do not like is a price we pay for an important freedom.

What is fatal to the trust and sense on which good broadcasting depends is outside intervention in the editorial process. *Deus ex machina* may be welcome at the end of the play. But divine intervention in the middle act can only devalue and destroy the main protagonists, or, at the very least, bind them together in anger against the jealous gods.

Annan reiterated that ultimate decisions in exceptional cases as to what may or may not be broadcast lie with the Authorities — at the BBC, the Board of Governors, in ITV, the Chairman and Members of the Independent Broadcasting Authority. What may we expect of them?

Not proximity: the further those asked to guard the public interest are removed from the making of the particular piece the better. Authorities over broadcasting work best when exercising a positive role, offering broad guidance, leaving broadcasters, if persuaded, to execute what they suggest: an old gap filled, growth nurtured, a new need met. The BBC's increased coverage of industry and business in recent years surely owes everything to a Board of Governor's initiative. A similar initiative on trade unions would now be equally welcome. And, in ITV, the IBA, whose detailed interventions created minor storms in too many 1970's tea cups, did much greater good by stealth by a stern insistence on maintaining the single play, extending current affairs, increasing documentary output, promoting arts coverage, sustaining and enlarging news, broadening, perhaps most markedly of all, the scope of drama series. (A single sentence in the published, critical appraisal of one company's performance made possible a transformation of its entire drama output.) If, in the commercial sector of our broadcasting system, there were no Broadcasting Authority, it would be necessary to invent one.

Supervisory broadcasting authorities must share the aspirations of the broadcaster. They must sympathise with the creative process. They must themselves feel the urge to publish. They are not to see their role as prevention only — 'Go next door. See what little Johnny is doing. Stop him'. They are not to strive never to offend. That is easy; stop all broadcasting. In extreme cases, even, they are to weigh their fear of getting it wrong against their positive duty to inform and entertain, stimulate, challenge, irritate, provoke. They represent the broadcaster to the audience as well as the audience, on occasion, to the broadcaster. Their members need to be aware of disparate interests, as well as of common bonds.

If, as agents of government, party or state, they see only the need to advance policy, avoid disturbance, secure conformity, then we are talking not of the regulation of broadcasting in democracies, but of repression in the tyrannical or would-be tyrannical state. The BBC's Board of Governors is of the BBC. The IBA is placed over a system of which ITV and ILR companies form part. Each is a supervisory body which should concern itself more with broad policy than with the day-to-day conduct of the editorial process. Yet they too need to share to the uttermost, indeed they need to articulate and embody the broad purpose of the broadcasters.

Authorities are not cheer leaders for those under them. They are there to relate what is done to social ends. They are there ultimately to regulate, else others will. But they also have positive roles. Both UK Authorities, co-existing for the future with a new Broadcasting Complaints Commission, will need to define those roles afresh.

Do we need Authorities at all? Is there any real justification for subjecting television and radio to restraints not imposed on newspapers, books, plays and scarcely at all in films? Given that an increasingly sophisticated citizenry relating always what they see and hear on television and radio, to what they experience in daily life, are increasingly free to choose to tune to varied sources, do they still need protection? Should anyone intervene between utterance and audience? Should there be a television channel, say, on which all who wish to speak or perform or persuade or sing or startle form an orderly queue?

Less need for Authorities' control, it is argued, as television channels breed, radio stations multiply, cassettes and cable proliferate, satellites loom over the horizon. But if these developments are not planned and controlled, Babel is built again. All will utter, none be heard or understood. Society is not to abdicate responsibility in the face of unrestrained technical growth.

The fourth British television channel is placed under the aegis of the IBA. It will draw its programme not just from the ITV companies, but from independent producers, working outside our present broadcasting institutions. The fourth channel will demonstrate whether, within the broad confines of the system that we have, it is possible to widen the range of voices that are heard, messages that are understood.

Authorities, making broad interventions, can achieve positive effects. A Communist state seeking to liberalise broadcasting, if such there were, could do worse than set up an independent Authority over it. Some democracies, where competition rules, are tentatively using the broadcasting Authority to attempt to tame market forces. Australia's use of the Broadcasting Commission to improve children's programmes is one current example. If there were ever an absolute political determination to achieve it, the balance of United States network output could be, modestly at any rate, affected also. In other democracies, like Israel, the Broadcasting Authority currently seeks to limit freedoms by imposing the will of Begin's Likud Government, which appointed it, on broadcasters who aspired and still aspire to be independent of the state.

In the United Kingdom the broadcasting authorities need to concentrate on great issues, seeking guarantees for the survival of the BBC, sustaining a social purpose in commercial television, supervising a new pluralism on a new channel, maintaining the balance of the whole. Theirs is a public trust. They must make public account of it.

The individual broadcaster will, inevitably, be concerned not with the whole, but with the particular. He has to find the language to speak of what he knows needs to be said. If he claims authority to speak, he too must be seen to deserve it.

NOTE

1. A system of 'approved schools' for juvenile offenders.

4 Janet Morgan

It was a great relief to hear that the Planning Committee for this symposium wanted to move communication studies away from communications specialists. That made me feel more relaxed, though, mind you, last week I realised I was better informed than some of my countrymen. I saw from a bus the Welsh Nationalist slogans painted on the base of Nelson's Column in Trafalgar Square. The first line read: 'Fourth Channel for Wales'. The second line was in Welsh and the third line read: 'Tories Betray . . .' and then petered out. An articulate middle-aged lady sitting behind me looked at her articulate middle-aged neighbour and said, 'Fourth channel for Wales. What do they want a fourth channel for? They haven't even got one yet'.

Now the chairman has mentioned his interest in the way in which major decisions about broadcasting are made by the exercise of political authority and he has said that it is very difficult to know how these decisions are taken. A distinguished television commentator, Huw Thomas, he reported, once said that he hoped 'the right chaps were in charge'; perhaps the most useful thing that I can do is to talk a bit about the chaps who are in charge in the United Kingdom and about political authority as it's exercised here, not only in the field of broadcasting but a lot of other fields. I shall outline a sketch of where authority lies within the government, particularly in regard to broadcasting matters. I shall not explore the formal details but, instead, offer more of a soufflé and I would like to emphasise that, although I will be talking very much about experience in the United Kingdom, perhaps some of my observations will remind those who are familiar with bureaucrats and politicians in other countries of characteristics that they display. Although I am talking about the present day, some of you will see historical parallels and, last, although I shall talk about politicians and bureaucrats, I am sure that you will recognise similar features in others who exercise authority — university vice-chancellors, programme control men, even industrial tycoons. (It *is* possible to imagine Lord Reith as the head of a commercial television company.) What I am sticking to is what you could call the *déformation professionel* of bureaucrats and politicians. I would like you to ask yourselves, if you would, whether the characteristics I will touch on are found in the people you know and encounter in politics and officialdom and whether you think any of these characteristics are found in broadcasters as well. I shall emphasise differences and conflicts — but you may wish to recall the similarities between politicians and bureaucrats, on the one hand, and journalists and broadcasters, on the other, and to remind me of their common problems. But I am not a visiting fireman; I shall try to be a visiting arsonist. I shall seek to pick up threads from previous discussions and tweak them a little bit.

Let us begin with officialdom. If you look at Weber's ideal type of bureaucracy, it has certain recognisable and constant features. First of all, there is an administrative structure. We are all familiar with those. Tasks are distributed and assigned to people who have certain functionally distinct offices. That distribution of tasks is relatively enduring. From time to time, admittedly, departments are changed and shuffled about and tasks are reassigned. Management consultants are called in and, if an organisation is centralised, they prescribe decentralisation and, if it is decentralised, they prescribe centralisation, but in the government bureaucracy in Britain the people who occupy those tasks and offices are generally 'permanently established'. They are, too, endowed with the requisite authority to carry out those tasks which have been assigned to them. Officials are trained to their jobs. (The word 'to' is interesting. Training is not necessarily 'for' a job. It may consist of working with another official who has already been performing the task in question for some time.) Officials are arranged in levels of rank and the rights that one rank has over another are specified by particular rules. An office-holder cannot and should not appropriate his office and its furnishings to his own use. He cannot use any influence he has to do favours for his friends just because they are his friends. The office's organisational resources are carefully distinguished from the private resources of office-holders.

The work in a bureaucracy of this ideal type consists in applying general rules to particular cases. The official does not go out of his way to favour or disfavour one applicant or another; he looks a rule up in the book and asks whether it applies here. And, last but very, very important, all transactions are recorded in files. There is an awful lot of writing done — masses and masses of paper — and it is stored, partly, of course, because bureaucrats rely upon precedent. (Remember I am describing an ideal type. Whether officials ever fish out those files and look at them or not is another matter.) Such a bureaucratic system is supposed to be 'instrumental'. It is set up in order to do certain things, to 'administer' — whatever that may be. But one of the most obvious results is that the perpetuation of the system tends to become an end in itself. Indeed, governments constantly try to reduce the numbers of officials and always stumble against this obstacle. It is very important to bear this point in mind when we consider what other speakers have said about the way in which authority vanishes. One way of losing recognised authority to perform a particular task is by appearing less interested in doing the task than in preserving the right to do it.

So there they are. These are the mandarins. They are hierarchical. They write things down and pass them to the next person up the tree, who will scribble notes on them and pass them to the next person up the tree. They are orderly, or so they think, and they work steadily, or so they think. In fact they are not really orderly or steady at all. As in the programme-makers' environment which Jeremy Isaacs has described, so in a government department there is all sorts of messiness and chaos. Moreover, officials are very possessive of the particular tasks assigned to them and this makes it very difficult to co-ordinate activity. Thus one bit of the Home Office deals with radio frequencies, and another bit deals with satellites, while a bit of the Foreign Office deals with the reactions of other countries to negotiations over radio frequencies and a bit of the Department of Industry deals with making satellites and selling them. Often each of the different bits doesn't know what another bit is doing or that another bit is doing anything at all. It's very, very difficult to break down such compartmentalism and possessiveness because in doing so the critic is threatening somebody's office, somebody's power and somebody's mystery. These are officials' secrets, this is their knowledge — of what is being done, why it's being done, where representations are coming from. They're not just *in* authority; they are also *an* authority on their particular subjects, and they're damned if they're going to share it.

Like Grace Wyndham Goldie's young producers, officials are imbued with a sense of professionalism. In many respects this is admirable. It's admirable, for instance, that on the 'Day of Action' (a recent, unsuccessful attempt to call a national strike) officials

should have been reading their government circulars explaining
that if they found that they really had to stay at home, couldn't get
into the office — indeed couldn't even report to local unemployment offices — if they found they had to do some of their work by
telephone and if the cost of those telephone calls outweighed the cost
of normal transportation to and from the office, then and only then
might they put in a claim for reimbursement. That is a tiny
example, but it is in such small ways and by means of such trifling
reminders that officials build up a constant awareness of 'public
accountability'.

There is no need for me to describe the special language officials
employ, with its extensive use of the passive voice ('It is regretted
that . . . '), buckpassing ('I am authorised to tell you . . . '),
circumlocution, acronyms and metaphors largely derived from
cricket ('Comments should be sent by close of play on
Monday . . . '). We are all familiar with its failings. Other
characteristics deserve more attention here. For instance, the
mandarins are obsessive, while holding to the notion that they are
pragmatic. They think they are not opinionated. They believe that
they are rational and they are proud of their judgement. Nonetheless they are subject to whim. Suddenly something is fashionable —
pay television, for example, or 'public access'. It is extraordinary
how officials will go overboard. Take school meals: one day it's meat
and two vegetables and the next day it's cabbage and nuts. They are
capable of passion but at the same time they believe they are cool.

Again, the mandarins believe that they understand and can
interpret the public interest, but they are at the same time cynical.
Indeed, they sometimes admit that those who make successful radio
or television programmes show much more skill than themselves at
discerning and responding to public tastes and needs — but,
simultaneously, the official mind cannot be wholly convinced that
this is so. Officials are irritated in a curiously indulgent way by the
glamour and frivolity of the lives that they believe that journalists
and broadcasters lead, an existence that is gaudy and seductive but
which seems to the official mind relaxed and ramshackle. Can such
exotic butterflies, the officials wonder, do more than give ephemeral
delight?

Let us now look at how officials make decisions. I emphasise that
we are of course talking about the top, where very large discretion is
vested in the mandarins. They have a great deal of authority on
certain subjects. It is also important to remember that decisions are

not orderly but muddled. Winning an argument partly depends on being able to write a paper faster than somebody else. Efforts to make the system orderly tend to exacerbate the confusion. For example, papers must be written and circulated forty-eight hours before they are to be discussed, first by meetings of officials who redraft them before they are circulated a further forty-eight hours before meetings of Ministers, where they are redrafted again. Such a scramble often produces arguments that are vague and based on unsupported assumptions, with lazy reasoning, bolstered by whatever facts and statistics happen to be to hand. I was glad that Lord Windlesham gave us his case study of the decision to show *Death of a Princess*, because it illustrates one of those rare cases where an observer can identify who within a bureaucratic hierarchy decided what should be done. In that case, a decision was taken within the bureaucratic pyramid of a television company, but a government bureaucracy is just the same. Most of the time the process of decision-making is much more confused and much more diffuse.

Officials believe that they are accountable to their Ministers and, indeed, in many respects they are. They believe deeply that their authority is legitimate. They have been appointed to their positions after rigorous examination and scrutiny and they are legitimated by the chain of accountability. As officials see it, their task is to advise Ministers, to give them a range of options, while bearing in mind the ideology and predilections of their Ministers and the statements of policy they have made. Thus officials seek to serve their masters as best they can and, if Ministers don't like the advice they receive, they can give other instructions. If the public or Parliament disapproves, Ministers will be told pretty quickly and remedies will be taken. That, anyhow, is the theory.

What about politicians? In many, though not all, respects, they're different from officials. Their lives are very bitty and distracted. They don't have just one task or a couple of tasks to do but they are doing dozens of things, often simultaneously and in a very great number of places — Parliament, the constituency (if they have one), the department and so on. The pace of their lives is unpredictable. There are perhaps *longueurs* but there are also periods of intense pressure and this goes on all day and often all night. Politicans have, and are chosen because they have, definite beliefs and opinions. Unlike officials, they are reticent neither by nature nor by profession. They talk all the time. And, unlike officials, they are not self-protective — in fact politicians are some of the most masochistic people it is possible to meet. You won't catch an official knocking on doors asking people whether they are going to vote for him. You won't catch an official standing up in a public square or at a meeting, at a party conference or before a pressure group, making speeches about government policy and knowing that he or she is going to receive abuse. Not only will you not catch officials going into the House of Commons and making speeches, but, when they do sit in the civil servants' box hearing their Ministers do so, they will afterwards confide, 'Well, I may not actually have thought very much of old so-and-so, my Minister, but, you know, you should hear that man standing up in the House of Commons, *making a speech*'. That to an official is a most extraordinary achievement. But this is what politicians seem to thrive on. They are, I suspect, insecure (they certainly have reason to be); they are in a hurry; they believe deeply that they are equipped to interpret desires — the desires of their constituents and the wider public. They see themselves as dedicated to setting agendas and describing, if no longer raising, expectations. Jeremy Isaacs has mentioned the theme of interpreting desires and has told us the story of the actor he met at the Serbian Institute who explained his particular skills by striking his stomach and saying, 'Mr Isaacs, I feel it *here*'. That, too, is where the politician feels his vocation.

Perhaps it is too glib to say that, whereas officials diminish expectations, politicians enlarge them, but as a broad generalisation it has some truth in it. And the other differences? Politicians are aware always of the majorities that are built out of minorities. They try to deal with a range of issues, not just those that, in the case of Ministers, concern their particular departments. Politicians are accountable, so they believe, for the general conduct of their government and their party as much as for their own specific decisions; criticism comes as much from abroad as from home. Nonetheless, in an important way, politicians and officials are temperamentally alike. Both lay great stress on legitimacy and accountability. Their authority is derived from different sources — election in the one case and appointment in the other — and it can be challenged in different ways. Still, and I emphasise that I am talking about British habits and traditions, the similarity remains: public legitimacy and public accountability together constitute the conscience of both bureaucrat and politician.

Now it is these two kinds of person who have authority to make decisions that affect broadcasting. They react upon each other in curious ways. They are frantic and also extremely slow, pulled back by inertia and delay. Legislation is always out of date. They are very earnest indeed but they have a sort of dotty ingenuity which from time to time borders on frivolity. Mad ideas erupt concerning, for example, possible rules for the wearing of seat belts or possible uses for the external broadcasting service. They have a message but they are paranoiacally secretive. The politicians react to the pressures of their various constituencies and officials to the pressures of their departmental clientèle but at the same time both are paternalist. They believe they know what is good for the public. They are afraid of interruption (and I will come to that in a second) but nonetheless arrogant — stand in the Central Lobby of the House of Commons or opposite the entrance to Horse Guards Parade and notice that important walk, hurrying, slightly hunched, shoulders dragged down by a heavy briefcase, brow furrowed by the cares of office, gazing, preoccupied, into the middle distance. Their lives are both routine and melodramatic. Much of their working day is devoted to taking pieces of paper from one side of a desk, scanning and initialling them, and putting them down on the other side, but some of those documents contain sentences that are fateful. The politicians' and officials' activity is both normal and cosmic.

Now, how do these characteristics affect their view of broadcasters? How do they think of you, or some of you? As a rule, politicians and officials don't understand the profession of broadcasting; apart from a handful of Ministers and Members of Parliament who formerly practised your profession, they don't know what you do all the time or how you do it. They don't really, I suspect, sympathise with what this Symposium has already described as the common purpose of broadcasting — the wish to publish. They see you as buccaneers, even a special variety of lounge lizard, people who often don't wear ties, who wear jeans to work. You are disorderly, you are unsteady, you too have your special baffling language. Moreover, you imitate tasks which politicians and officials traditionally think of as their own — staging debates, putting arguments, interpreting the public interest, having opinions, initiating ideas as well as reporting them. In the eyes of the politician and official, the broadcaster has to a large extent usurped or tried to usurp much of what they have customarily regarded as their office, their authority.

Further, they think of you as slippery, counsel as well as witness. They are very, very well aware of your power; they sense that not only have you a medium which they themselves desperately need but also that you often have messages to put — and you are better at it than they are themselves. Admittedly, politicians and officials try, albeit warily, to learn how to present themselves and their explanations on radio and television. It is touching — and illuminating — to read the official handbooks describing how best to do so; the authors are all too plainly aware that their readers must be coaxed into facing the microphone and the camera, that they must be patiently taught to learn new techniques and adapt old ones.

But, from the politicians' and officials' point of view, the broadcasters' worst sin is that they make life even more difficult and complicated. Broadcasters are wild cards. They interrupt what is in any case a frenzied life, not only with sudden crises, like the Carrickmore episode or *Death of a Princess*, but also with constant daily and nightly pressures. Broadcasters *want* things — money, licence, facts, interviews — and they give a platform to other people who want other things — redress, change, attention. Officials are asked by their political masters to collect views, very carefully, and together both seek to come gradually to a judgement; suddenly some broadcaster jumps the gun. In their eyes, broadcasters are not time-savers but time-wasters, increasing rather than reducing burdens. Tensions and difficulties will thus inevitably arise between politicians and officials on the one hand and journalists and broadcasters on the other.

It is to contain these that various sorts of regulatory apparatus have been established: charters and statutes devised to give as large a measure of freedom as possible and simultaneously to impose constraints. In this respect, the BBC and the IBA are treated just like any other public body. The same sort of pressures and conflicts arise, particularly over money and appointments, with, for instance, the nationalised industries or the universities and research councils. Similarly, in each case a regulatory system is framed to ease the unavoidable discomforts of the relationship.

How do the political and official authorities try to cope with the strain of their relationship with the broadcasting authorities? The last thing politicians and officials want is to censor broadcasters. They realise how detrimental to their own authority would be any evidence, even rumour, that they have sought to edit broadcast material or to put pressure on broadcasting organisations. They know they must turn their backs on the enticing but dangerous path of editorial interference. Nevertheless, they are obliged to take an interest in what is broadcast and how and, as we have seen, they are anxious to minimise the complications of their own working lives. How can this be done? There are all sorts of ways: by setting up a regulated monopoly or by bringing in competition. Or somehow or other a system of checks and balances can be created. Or the government can leave broadcasters alone; I'm sure you all know the famous verse:

> You cannot hope to bribe or twist
> Thank God! the British journalist.
> But seeing what the man will do
> unbribed, there's no occasion to.

For most of the time there is no reason why the government should feel it necessary to interfere. Overall, 'balance' is achieved. What happens when the government does feel obliged to intervene? Jeremy Isaacs has described 'the doctrine of the two telephone calls': at least two telephone calls must be made to the broadcasting authority in question by which ever political or official authority is seeking to forestall or influence the transmission of an item. 'Sometimes', Mr Isaacs reminded us, 'those calls work and sometimes they don't work, because only one of them is connected'. The freedom of British broadcasting is protected because rules are not explicit and complete and because both government and broadcasting authorities enjoy a large measure of discretion as to how, if at all, they will use their several powers. There are doubtless politicians and officials who try to ensure that, when they try the second call, they ring the wrong number. They don't necessarily want to get through.

There are other ways by which the government can avoid the alluring trap of interfering with broadcasting. For instance, the terms of an argument can be skilfully changed: instead of objecting to the content of programmes, the authorities can remind broadcasters of historical analogies, of cases where other broadcasters found it politic to show self-restraint. Rather than discussing the size of the BBC licence fee or of the subsidy to the External Services in terms which suggest that government decisions will curb the broadcasters' resources, emphasis can be placed on the need to check public expenditure generally in a time of dearth. The government cannot entirely sever its connection with the broadcasting authorities, not least because those same citizens who treasure a free broadcasting system will from time to time press the government to put the broadcasters' house in order. Politicians can, however, circumscribe their intervention. They can be strictly jealous of the power to take part in certain, obviously relevant decisions: the number and nature of political broadcasts, for example, the form of election coverage, the broadcasting of Parliamentary proceedings and the discussion of Members' interests. But, by and large, politicians and officials prefer *not* to intrude. They seek to appoint safe people, who can be left to ensure that 'things are got right'. They look to market solutions. They hope that new technology will perhaps change the relationship between government and broadcasters, or even make regulatory problems so very, very complicated that the government has to abandon any attempt to deal with them at all.

This is why it is particularly important for us to consider what sort of regulatory apparatus British broadcasting will need in the next decade. None of these problems are new. During this conference we have discussed the persistently difficult relationship between the government and the press. Asa Briggs has described its complexities in the early nineteenth century and Anthony Smith has reminded us of the quarrels of the nineteenth and twentieth centuries. The attitudes of politicians and officials towards the Press at that time may not be so very unlike their attitudes to radio and television broadcasters today.

From time to time, of course, conflict worsens. We can identify at least three reasons why at this moment the relationship is under special strain. First of all, the cohesion of our society has been eroded. We are very conscious of social, economic and ideological divisions, of ethnic, regional, sexual and generational differences of view. Radio and television remind us of these, presenting clashes starkly, while the government authorities seek to encourage a sense of national unity. Secondly, there is a prevailing feeling of economic and political failure. Politicians and officials realise that, when citizens feel that the legitimate authorities are incompetent, they will turn elsewhere for guidance, to those who seem better informed, more competent, more responsive, although, constitutionally, their authority is illegitimate. Radio and television offer one of the most effective and respectable means for challenging legitimate but impotent authorities, and the broadcasters' role is accordingly resented by those who traditionally acted as the public's guide and chaperone.

The third, and last, reason for the deterioration of the relationship has to do with information. For a very long time politicians and officials have believed that they know what people want, whether they should have it, how they might be given it and what the price will be. More, the government has hitherto had a very much greater amount of information than anyone else or any other body. Now, however, journalists and broadcasters possess a great deal of information too, which may come from different groups in society and may be a different sort of information from that which the government has acquired. It may not tell the same story; it may arrive and be published earlier. Often the facts that broadcasters obtain concern issues about which the government authorities are especially sensitive — police corruption, for instance, political compromise, administrative inefficiency, Northern Ireland. Friction and suspicion grow where each group believes that the other has information that it lacks itself and where there is no communication between the two groups. One side is exasperated by the government's habits of official secrecy and official anonymity; the other is maddened by the broadcasters' determination not to jeopardise editorial independence or betray the confidentiality of sources.

If these conflicts and tensions are inevitable and if we agree that there is some likeness between my caricatures of politicians, officials and broadcasters and the actual occupants of these offices, what are we going to do about it? One course is to look at international comparisons. Are there other ways of recruiting, training and employing officials, politicians and broadcasters? How can they learn to appreciate the choices that members of other professions have to make, to understand different styles of operation, to see that those who exercise other forms of authority are as equally burdened with a sense of responsibility? We need a lot more openness, a lot more awareness. In Karl Deutsch's phrase, 'We are engaged on a search operation'. We also want a lot more satire and ridicule. The fools and jesters, mentioned by Asa Briggs, should not be dissuaded from mocking the inadequacies and idiosyncrasies of all those who enjoy a measure of power — the broadcasting organisations as much as the government authorities. Last of all, we must remember that maybe there is no such thing as 'truth'. It is not only impossible to establish a 'true account' of an event or a 'true view' of how things are; it is also impossible and impracticable to attribute to any authority a monopoly of knowledge and wisdom. The authorities who realise this have, surely, the best chance of survival.

5 Dennis Lawrence

For the civil servant concerned with the administration of the government's interest in broadcasting, the question of authority starts from the need to manage the allocation and use of radio frequencies. By Act of Parliament and by international treaty, this is a matter for the government; and the need for that management is indisputable. To use Lord Reith's evocative and time-touched phrase, someone must be 'the policeman of the aether'; and it cannot be anyone else. Authority here is uncomplicated: government, through an executive Department of State, licenses the use of frequencies. Broadly, its concern will be to make the most intensive possible use of the frequencies available under international agreement to the United Kingdom. As the licenser, it will seek to ensure that its licensees observe conditions prescribed to prevent, or to reduce to generally acceptable levels, interference by one transmission with any other. It is concerned essentially with the means, and not the ends; with the signal and not the message it contains. But when the signal is broadcast for general reception, when the licence authorises the licensee to address mass audiences in this country and in others, when in short the messages become television and radio programmes, then the consequences of the act of licensing become different in kind. They become social. And unless some special and convincing measure were taken to relieve Ministers of the responsibility, sooner or later they would be expected to answer not only for the technical behaviour of their licensees, their observance of the conditions attaching to the means of transmission: they would be expected to use the licence so as to provide that the programmes as a whole were 'balanced' — that is, wide-ranging enough in their subject matter; and that programme items were 'fair' or 'decent' or 'truthful'. This is not, certainly in this country and in the western democracies generally the government's business. The special and convincing measure taken to keep it from becoming the government's business was the creation of the broadcasting authority, the public corporation to act as the custodian of the public interest in broadcasting defined as the messages, the programmes transmitted. It is upon that part of the relationship between the government and the broadcasting authorities which reflects the general and continuing attention paid to them as the providers of the programmes, that interest focuses; and it is to the conduct as I saw it from 1959 to 1973 of that part of the relationship that this account is directed.

Focus of attention certainly, but not by any means the whole story; and there is some risk that my account will be read as implying an almost exclusive interest in that one aspect. The reality was quite otherwise; and though my official interest in broadcasting lasted longer than is usual, it was still less than half the time needed to carry through from conception to completion the immense task of changing the line definition standard from 405 to 625 lines, the main but by no means the only technical development of the period. To provide a corrective, let me sketch what this required: international agreement on the deployment and use of ultra-high frequencies; the creation of a chain of co-sited BBC and IBA UHF transmitting stations to duplicate on 625 lines the 405-line services already transmitted to virtually the whole country on very high frequencies; the continuance of the VHF transmissions until the population coverage attained by the UHF transmissions was complete enough and until viewers had stopped using 405-line sets; and the timely design first of dual-standard 405/625-line–VHF/UHF receivers and secondly, of single-standard 625-line UHF receivers. It involved departments of government, broadcasting organisations and industry — both the set and the equipment manufacturers. It needed much devoted and co-ordinated effort by all three to carry the project through. And from conception in the early 1950s to completion marked by the cessation — now expected in the mid-1980s — of the 405-line transmissions, it will have taken more than thirty years: seven Parliaments so far, and seven administrations — four Conservative and three Labour. A remarkable achievement, but little remarked; and one which, in my time, occupied a lot of it.

Important though the technical means are, the programmes are the ends; and both the BBC and the IBA are public corporations created on the proposal of the government with the approval of Parliament to provide television and radio programmes. A constitutional invention designed to fill the need for a form of organisation to pursue activities which are better not left to private initiative nor undertaken by the government itself, the public corporation draws its authority from the statute or other legal instrument bringing it into being. The range of the activities undertaken by public corporations, including as they do the nationalised industries and the development agencies, is wide and varied. Yet they are all constituted in essentially the same way, and stand in essentially the same relationship to the government. In summary, they are independent of the government in the day-to-day conduct of their affairs and they are therefore liable to answer for their operational performance not to Ministers or Departments of State but to Parliament before which their annual reports must be laid by Ministers to whom they send them, and before which they may be — and regularly are — called to account for their performances. The first duty of the government is to appoint and if need be dismiss the Chairmen and other members of the corporations. In discharging that duty, the government's concern is to try to ensure that the corporations are composed of people who will satisfactorily carry out the responsibilities entrusted to them. Ministers do not answer for the operation of the enterprises in the charge of corporations, but they do for the competence of the men and women they have appointed to them.

In a debate about programme content, a Postmaster General in a Labour Government put the point thus of the Chairman and Governors of the BBC, and the Chairman and Members of what was then still the ITA: 'You back them, or sack them; but you do not muck them about', a pronouncement later described by a Minister of Posts and Telecommunications in a Conservative Government as an impeccable statement of constitutional doctrine. For completeness, however, let us note that a Minister may be asked Questions in Parliament on any matter for which he is responsible; so that where he has powers of general or specific direction, or to require information, Members of Parliament may ask him about his use of the powers or press him to make use of them. That the power of direction is in the particular case a reserve power does not preclude Questions.

Thus, each of the broadcasting authorities has had conferred on it full formal authority to provide broadcasting services and has had imposed on it the concomitant liability to check by Parliament. Parliament has given some guidance on what its expectations are. The services are to be provided as public services for the dissemination of information, education and entertainment. The programmes are to maintain a high general standard in all respects, and in particular, in respect of their content and quality, and a proper balance and wide range in their subject matter. As far as possible nothing is to offend against good taste or decency or to be liable to incite to crime, or to lead to disorder or to be offensive to public feeling. As far as possible news programmes are to be presented with due accuracy and impartiality. As far as possible, programmes dealing with matters of political or industrial controversy or relating to current public policy are to preserve due impartiality. And so on. All this must be read as very largely, if not wholly, hortatory. It is not and cannot be a definition of good broadcasting. It cannot be because what constitutes good broadcasting is too much a matter of opinion, or of moral or aesthetic judgement.

Parliament did, in fact, consider whether it should try to go further. When the Television Act 1964 was in Committee of the House of Commons, an opposition spokesman proposed to write into it some words taken from Chapter 3 of the Pilkington Report. That chapter was, both Government and Opposition agreed, an authentic statement of aims and objectives. With the enthusiasm admissible in opposition, their spokesman declared it to be one of the finest chapters he had seen in a public document. With the sobriety required of responsibility, the government spokesman declared it to be an excellent exposition of the purposes of broadcasting. The words to be written in were culled from paragraph 49, and declared it to be the broadcasting authorities' duty to respect the public's right to choose from the widest possible range of subject matter and so to enlarge worthwhile experience. That the programmes should contain a wide range was, in fact, prescribed. The rest, which is not about matter but purpose, was rejected by the government side. Not because they thought it wrong in a statement of the purposes that a service of broadcasting should seek to serve; on the contrary, they accepted it. It was not however the stuff of which statutes were made. On the understanding that the statement represented the government's expectations of the aims to which the Authority's performance would be directed, the opposition withdrew its amendment. So, though the full statement never saw the light of statutory day, it remains an agreed view of Parliament's intention.

We are left, then, with this: that the full definition of a satisfactory service of broadcasting is a matter of operational practice, and for the broadcasting authorities to determine and redetermine. By their deeds we are to know them. If they fail to meet the expectations viewers and listeners have of them, they will lose the authority they derive from satisfactory performance. They are subject to the continuing check of opinion, in all the ways that it expresses itself: in the press, by lobbies claiming to represent the general or a particular interest, but finally and pre-eminently, in Parliament.

So far, so simple and so good. But what is the practice, as distinct from the precept, really like? There are the accounts one reads alleging a ministerial or official disposition if not an actual attempt to interfere, to decide the content of programmes. And they are often asked to intervene. The word is 'interference' when the action, real or imaginary, is deprecated, and 'intervention' when it is advocated. What about the arm-twisting which, if the reports are right, the Chairmen of the politically interesting public corporations regularly endure at the hands of Ministers and their officials: surely the broadcasters are no less liable to it? The short answer is that, in a free society, just as the broadcasters must attend to opinion, so too may they appeal to it: to the press, to the lobbies and to Parliament. Arguably, an appeal to Parliament against a government which — and this is usually the case — can command a majority in the House of Commons, is a dubious safeguard. Still, the broadcasters can turn to 'Her Majesty's Loyal Opposition'; and a government would have to be very certain that it could justify intervention on the ground that the public interest required it. For the independence of the broadcasting authorities is, in a country without a written constitution, a constitutional fact.

That is the short answer. But there is more to it. Some years ago I discussed with the Chairman of a major and politically interesting public corporation the question of independence. He took it as read that the relationship between government and public corporation could not be wholly explained by reference to the formal prescription, that within a necessarily general framework there had to be pressures and counter-pressures, checks and balances; that if his organisation did not attend to opinion, whether by explaining or justifying its policies and practices, or by changing them, Ministers could themselves come under pressure to intervene; and that ultimately they might feel compelled to do so. But it was, he argued, easier for the broadcasting authorities; for surely virtually everyone accepted that it was not the government's business to decide what news should be presented, what opinions heard, what tastes approved. That was why the broadcasting authorities were independent. Yet, on reflection, not quite: it was why they *should be*. There was the matter of money. For each of the broadcasting authorities, its money was its own, to apply in promoting its objects; and the policy of each was to pay out of income for capital developments. Therefore neither broadcasting authority added to the public sector borrowing requirement; and the government was banker to neither and hence could not have a banker's prudential interest in the conduct by either of its affairs. Upon these considerations finally depended the fact of the broadcasting authorities' independence of the government. In other words, the methods of financial provision must be consistent with the intention, with the Parliamentary intention, that the government should not interfere. Or intervene. Or muck them about.

For independent broadcasting, earning its money by the sale of advertising time, that consistency is self-evident. For the BBC it needs explaining. To avoid the heresy of hypothecated taxation, the money paid to the BBC to run the Home Services[1] is not 'the licence money' but a grant paid out of moneys voted by Parliament to the Secretary of State and equal to the net licence revenue. How then can it be said that the grant is the BBC's money, is its own to spend as it thinks fit? The formal answer is that though conditions may be attached by Parliament or the Treasury to the grant, no such conditions have been attached. Parliament leaves it unconditionally to the BBC to spend on its objects the money granted. To quote from a memorandum submitted in January 1969 by the General Post Office, then a Department of Government:

> It is precisely because the amount paid to the BBC from the Consolidated Fund is related to the net licence revenue that the Corporation are not subject to the same kind of detailed control as is a Government Department. The licence fee system contains its own financial discipline. Any significant increase in potential revenue only derives from an increase in the fee: and the Corporation cannot expect increases too often. In effect, the BBC have to persuade Government that it would be right to ask viewers and listeners to pay more. There is thus in the mind of the public a direct relationship between the services provided by the BBC and the amount of the licence fee.

In plainer words, whatever dodges Whitehall may devise to see that the proceeds of a particular source of revenue are not directed to a specific pocket, people know that they are paying for the BBC. So they are prompted to ask if they are getting value for money, and the BBC whether it is giving it. Money as a medium of exchange exercises its two-way discipline: on the buyer to consider whether and how much he wants to buy, and on the seller to supply efficiently. There is not the same direct financial relationship between independent broadcasting, and viewers and listeners; nor, given the method of financing it, is any special pronouncement needed to establish its independence of the government.

There are other consequences. One is that, when the period of their contracts has expired, the programme companies' performance comes under scrutiny by the IBA. In effect, they are called to account for the use of their delegated authority; and it may or may not be renewed. Another is the effect on the level of expectation the public have of the services, what the broadcasting organisations' performance must be to deserve and keep the authority conferred on them. An eminent acquaintance in whose many-sided life golf was — after his family and his profession — the third passion, telephoned me one morning to ask briskly how a public service of television could, in order to show some advertisements, cut off the climactic conclusion of a game. A man accustomed to obedience in others, he brushed aside my objection that the Authority and not the Minister was responsible for programme content. There followed a leading question put as though by Counsel for the prosecution to a witness for the defence: what was my view? He did not think well of what I had to say. It was he and the viewing public who were being mucked about. But he had no real expectation that such a tidal wave of indignation would surge through the Palace of Westminster as to compel Members of Parliament by the dozen to put their names to a motion deploring the whole reprehensible business. And he was right: there was not so much as a ripple. Viewers and listeners do not look their broadcasting gift horses so closely in the mouth as they do those they pay for directly.

Therefore the Parliamentary intention that, subject to the check of opinion, full authority should reside in the broadcasting organisations, is made actual by methods of finance, which in turn act upon the public expectation of the broadcasting services. Suppose, though, that there is a more general and continuing concern or annoyance about programme content culminating, say, in a persistent succession of Questions asking Ministers to use their powers to veto a programme or class of programmes, or that a broadcasting authority's plans for making changes in the character of its services are attracting widespread criticism. Suppose that the degree of concern, annoyance or criticism may be approaching the point where it would question whether the practical realisation by a broadcasting authority of the objects of the public services matched the public, and in particular, Parliamentary expectation. And suppose further that the broadcasting authority is apparently failing to attend to that developing opinion either by explaining or justifying its practice or proposals convincingly, or by altering them. Potentially, the situation is one in which the competence of those appointed by Ministers as trustees for the public interest in the services might be questioned. Hence, it is also one on which the government is bound to take a view. In order to do so, it needs to assess, on the one hand, the force of the criticism and, on the other, the problems facing the broadcasting authority. Inescapably, the Minister responsible is cast in a mediating role. If he is to perform it, there must be a continuing dialogue between him and the broadcasting authorities. That dialogue is mainly conducted on his behalf with the staff of the BBC and the IBA, by the civil servants advising him. At the one extreme is the simple enquiry made so that a letter can be answered, the answer reiterating, if need be, that as the programmes are the broadcasting authority's business, the complaint or criticism has been brought to its attention. At the other extreme, the dialogue may comprehend an exposition of proposals for making major changes in the range and character of the services, changes such as would constitute in effect a redefinition by the broadcasting authority of what was needed to provide a service of good broadcasting, excite controversy, and call for a personal exchange between the Minister and the Chairman.

Lord Hill has published an account[2] of the controversy which in 1969 attended the BBC's plans for radio in the 1970s, an account showing the relationship in operation at all its stages. First, there was the formulation by the Corporation of its proposals for major changes in the character and structure of the radio services. Next came discussions with Ministers about the financial and political implications, this stage continuing in parallel with the third, the publication of the proposals and the crystallisation by the press and in Parliament of opinion about them. There were two debates, one in the House of Commons on 22 July and one—in February 1970 — in the House of Lords, the government's task being to justify the ways of the BBC to man, and to respond to what man had to say about the ways of the BBC: in short, to mediate. The controversy was marked by the emergence of a separate body of protest calling itself the Campaign for Better Broadcasting, supported by programme producers employed by the BBC. Part of its case was that the Corporation's administrators were out of sympathy with the aspirations of the producers and that this constituted a threat to the standards of broadcasting. As administrators ourselves, and at one stage further removed from the essential business of broadcasting, the production of the programmes, we officials found the allegation instructive. After observing that in part the internal misgivings stemmed from fear rather than fact, Lord Hill concludes: 'Although I realised that often a charge of failure adequately to consult really means a failure to accept the views of those consulted, in this case there seemed to be substance in the criticisms'. If there had been some failure of imagination by the Corporation's administrators, so that somehow they had not fully entered into the minds and feelings of those who know most about making programmes and mostly love what they know, how inadequate might our perception be of this among the broadcasting organisations' own problems.

Evidently the diplomatic aspect of the relationship between the broadcasting authorities and the government cannot be provided for by formal prescription. Necessary though it is, it is perhaps the most difficult to practise and to explain: difficult to practise because the distinction between the approach made by the government as the body which may have to justify in the face of external criticism the appointments it has made, and the approach made by the government as a party directly interested on grounds of public policy in the content of a particular programme may not always be clear; difficult to explain because, since most people have better things to do than study the small print of such a constitutional relationship, there is a natural public disposition to regard the diplomacy with scepticism. And whether they are for intervention or against interference, the sceptics will be at one in their scepticism. None of this is to say that the government should not or may not complain, if it considers that it has cause. No one need suspect intervention, or covert censorship, when it does so publicly, for its appeal is then to public opinion, and opinion will judge whether the government or the broadcasting authority is in the right. But it may prefer to make its complaint privately; and the preference might be justifiable. It is still for the broadcasting authority to decide whether or not to defer to the government's view. That is not, of course, the end of the road. There remains the government's power of veto. And, finally and essentially, there remains the broadcasting authority's right to state publicly that its power of veto has been used.

Recently, Sir Michael Swann observed that this right was all the BBC had to resort to if the power of veto were in fact used. All, and yet everything:[3] for again, the effect is to compel an appeal to public, and so to Parliamentary, opinion. No government would use the power unless it were sure that opinion would support it decisively. Neither broadcasting authority would, by failing to consider other than very earnestly an appeal by the government not to broadcast something, risk the exercise of the power of veto where opinion was likely to see that use as justified. In a country where freedom of expression is a right, the onus of proof bears much more heavily on those who would wish to suppress than it does on those who would publish and not be damned. And, in fact, no particular programme has ever been vetoed.

Here, then, in the unprescribed relationship is the interface where the authority of the government and that of the broadcasting authorities meets, and where the constitutional structure is tested. There must, of course, be held in common certain basic assumptions: that the medium should be used positively to extend awareness; that it should try to show the whole range of experience — fun and games no less than exaltation; that it should pay special attention to the experimental and novel; and above all, that the public's right to choose from the widest range of subject matter should be respected. It is one of the values of the independent committee of enquiry into broadcasting that, just as it affords an opportunity for a more detailed and searching examination than would otherwise be possible of the performance of the broadcasting authorities, so it must make an informed pronouncement about objectives and standards. That pronouncement has itself to pass the test of opinion. If it does so, it stands until supplanted as a statement to which all may refer — or, better, may keep in mind — as a more extended and perceptive view than it is possible to make in the legal instruments of the public expectations the broadcasters should seek to satisfy. As we have seen, Chapter 3 of the Pilkington Report commanded — as, I gather, it still commands — general assent.

It provided a framework of assumptions within which to conduct the Minister's mediating function. Do not suppose that exchanges between the Minister and his advisers on the one hand, and the broadcasting authorities on the other, or between the Minister and Members of Parliament, would start by quoting a text; indeed, a direct reference would be rare. It was rather that the general thrust and purport of Chapter 3 was taken as given. There were differences of emphasis, quirks, blind-spots: an interface is never frictionless. But the essential ingredients, a shared understanding of the authenticated purposes of broadcasting, and good-will were there.

So it was roses, roses pretty well all the way? No, of course not. Now and then we fell upon the thorns of life and bled a little. For programmes are broadcast which on any objective view, if often one seen with hindsight, must be supposed to damage the national interest, or give offence. I illustrate the point by reference to more recent examples because they will be more vividly in mind. Whether one applauds the programme as a fearless attempt to show the truth for what it is or condemns it as ultimately but essentially meretricious, the wider consequences of Independent Television's *Death of a Princess* cannot be dismissed as trifling. Nor can the view that the BBC's series of four programmes 'Law and Order' was unfair to judges, prison doctors, police, prison warders—and possibly to others. Here, the reply given by Lord Harris answering on 8 May 1979 for the government and as Home Office Minister to a Question tabled by Lord Gordon-Walker, is especially interesting for the sharp distinction it drew between the department's responsibilities for the services portrayed in the series, and its role as custodian of the constitutional relationship between the government and the broadcasting authorities. Asked by Lord Gordon-Walker whether the government proposed to make representations to the BBC about the programme, Lord Harris replied to the effect that the Secretary of State had made a public expression of his concern but that the government did not intend to depart from the long-established policy of non-intervention in matters of programme content.

Then there is the concern some have felt about the reporting of events in Northern Ireland. Again, one may judge on the one hand that the reports are no more than a responsible attempt to bring the reality of the situation there to general attention. Or one may judge that the character and content of the reporting have sometimes owed more to competitive shock-mongering. I do not suppose for one moment that any broadcaster consciously decides: 'Our news must be more exciting than theirs'. But the competitive pressure being there, the need is consciously to guard against the unconscious adoption of such a response to it, a response which will progressively corrupt news values. If, after the clamour has died down, opinion settles in such cases as these to the second of the views one may take of them, then the broadcasting organisation's moral stock will have been diminished, and with it the respect it must retain as a condition of the authority entrusted to it.

Therefore, there arise, inevitably, causes for public concern on which Ministers must take a view. People who work in the broadcasting organisations are fallible and at the best there will be some failures of judgement; at the worst there will be a failure to live up to the moral imperative which lies at the heart of the broadcaster's business: to tell the truth as far as he can portray it. The ways in which such a failure may show are many. It may, for example, be by use of the documentary forms to confuse fact with fiction; by the appeal to salacity in a programme presented as a critical examination of social or cultural attitudes; in news and news commentary programmes, by the tendency to prefer exciting visual material and so either to reduce or exclude items which are more important and more newsworthy, but less televisual; or, by trying to give them a spurious televisual quality, to exaggerate or even to misrepresent. Emphatically the medium is not the message.

As emphatically, I must not be read as having regarded it as remotely part of my task to be Whitehall's programme watcher, waiting with anticipatory and jaundiced eye for trouble to turn up. My point is that the mediating role, implicit in the authority vested in the government to appoint those who have a right and duty to provide public services of broadcasting, requires it to understand both the critic and the criticised. So the mediator is bound to recognise that such failures are first an abuse of the broadcasting medium; and there will be more dismay on that account among production staff, among the creative people for whom broadcasting is an art, their art, than among those who take upon themselves the role of public censor of broadcasting but take as their prime purpose the suppression of prurience. If only morality in broadcasting were so simple and so certain. If only those who most readily pronounce upon it were not so certain and simplistic. And, secondly, such failures are an abuse of the trust confided in the broadcasting authorities along with the authority conferred upon them: the trust of viewers and listeners.

All that about the broadcasting authority's half of the interface; what about the other half, the civil servants'? Those who were informed, educated and entertained by the series *Yes, Minister* and were satisfied that the programmes told the whole story will know that in every Minister there is a well-meaning romantic struggling to get out, that in each of his advisers a self-safety-first expert contrives to prevent the escape, and that there is no more to be said. Those who took the conventions of the genre as given and suspended disbelief were entertained by a series which directed some timely but never malicious mockery at Whitehall. Also, they will have been informed and educated, just a little; but their disbelief now unsuspended, they will know that there is a lot more to it. For an external view of the civil servants' performance at the interface, you have to turn to the broadcasting authorities and, especially to their administrators. They have to deal with us. But I can say what I feared that our failure might be, what we would need consciously to guard against, and that was a failure of imagination. This might happen in two main ways. Our comprehension of the characteristics of broadcasting, and of television in particular, as a medium of communication, our perception of its possibilities and limitations might be inadequate. The second was that we would not sufficiently reckon with the broadcasting organisations' obligation to the medium's creators and innovators, to its need to foster and encourage, to give new voices a hearing, to look for new perceptions, to challenge conventions. All publishers have to make choices and it would be fatally easy for the broadcasters to settle for a play-safe policy. No-one but those whose business it is to commission programme material and produce programmes can, I suspect, fully know what demands the job conscientiously done will impose at the extreme; to balance judgements of aesthetic or educative value and integrity of purpose against care for the feelings of the individual men and women contained in audiences of millions. My concern was that the natural disposition of Whitehall would lead us to conduct our side of the relationship without sufficient allowance for the need to experiment and adventure, without sufficient under-standing of the obligations the administrators in broadcasting have to those who make up its creative force. I took much comfort from the last two sentences of Chapter 3:

All broadcasting and television especially, must be ready and anxious to experiment, to show the new and unusual, to give a hearing to dissent. Here, broadcasting must be most willing to make mistakes; for if it does not, it will make no discoveries.

That was what Parliament had affirmed. That showed where the benefit of the doubt must lie.

Granted the recognition that mistakes will be made, the broadcasting organisations were too reluctant to say so when they had. That mistakes will occur is a *condition* of a good service of broadcasting. An oversensitive reaction to criticism is bound to make the mediator's task more difficult. Turning away from the hurt broadcaster to the indignant critic, the mediator knows that he can neither explain nor mollify. The broadcasting organisations have, of course, to reckon with the morale of production staff. Their public disposition is bound to be to defend and protect them. This we recognised and tried to allow for in full. But it remains my judgement that they would have done better to say more readily and more graciously: 'We were wrong'. If justification disarms a critic, admission of mistake will usually prompt him to put his weapon down. If he gets neither the one nor the other he keeps it up: after all, the offender might do it again. Perhaps though my recollection reflects a failure of the civil servant's imagination, that even after the reaction of producers to *Broadcasting in the Seventies* we did not fully take the measure of the broadcasting organisations' difficulty. My plea in mitigation would then be that they might have tried harder to explain themselves. The apology tendered by the BBC to Mr Harold Wilson to resolve the dispute caused by the broadcast of *Yesterday's Men* is described by Lord Hill[4] as grudging; and since the apology sought is described in his account as abject and as supported by threat of legal action, perhaps that had to be the outcome. A pity, all the same.

Finally, a look at the future. There is in prospect, and if we choose to pay for it, a proliferation of the number of television channels. It would not necessarily follow from their provision that there would be more choice of programme material. To suppose otherwise would be not a failure of imagination, but a failure of intelligence. The fact is already there, and has been for more than a decade, for anyone to see in other parts of the world, most notably in North America; and it is that an increase in the number of channels may very well enable the viewer to see more of less on each of them, and the same on all. When it is suggested, as it has been recently, that by the end of the century a multiplicity of channels will have made what has been called 'this anguished balancing of freedom and control by a broadcasting authority' a thing of the past, one is bound to wonder whether there is not in that observation an element of wishfulness born out of administrative fatigue. For the anguish can only be that of the administrator doing the balancing and getting tired of it, not of a producer with a sense of vocation, with a conviction that his business is to contribute to the purposes of broadcasting, to help make real the possibility of using the medium to minister to the public's right to choose from the widest possible range of subject matter and so to enlarge worthwhile experience. And whether television comes to us over many channels or few, by broadcast transmission or wire-distribution network, it will still bring into our homes working models of human behaviour. If there is more to broadcasting than trade, if we consider that the power that goes with its use should not go without responsibility, then we shall continue to need broadcasting authorities answerable to Parliament. In the strict sense of the word, the services of broadcasting provided in this country are generally excellent; by common consent they excel those provided in others. It would be silly to put that achievement at risk, silly and perhaps dangerous. The reasons for diminishing the role of the broadcasting authorities might be political, that their activity was after all one over which the government should exercise more control, or even undertake; or commercial, and so should be left to the private initiative. If a choice ever had to be made between the two, there can be no doubt that in a free society it could only be for the second; for the first alternative is sinister. Broadcasting is too important, much too important, not to be left to the broadcasters.

NOTES

1. Home Services means all the services of radio and television broadcasting for general reception in the United Kingdom, and is so distinguished from the External Services, which is separately financed.
2. Lord Hill of Luton, *Behind the Screen: the broadcasting memoirs of Lord Hill of Luton* (Sidgwick & Jackson, 1974), pp. 126–46.
3. Annan argues persuasively that the express power of veto, subject to check by publication, is preferable to no power at all — and that it gives the broadcasters greater security from undue pressure.
4. *Behind the Screen*, pp. 190–1.

6 Randolph Quirk

Speaking into the Air

When Edmund Burke seized upon the idea of the press as the fourth estate (implying equal power with the Commons, the Lords, and the Church), he was helping to elevate the media to a position far above their station.[1] When the *Times Educational Supplement* in 1932 called radio the fifth estate, a still greater flattery was perpetrated, and the BBC has needed little encouragement to try and live up to it. In this spirit, Andrew Timothy, following a month's scrutiny of radio output, concludes that 'the BBC has a clear duty to uphold the standards of spoken English',[2] a plea that seeks support from an unattributed quotation in the form of a resounding rhetorical question: 'For if the trumpet give an uncertain sound, who shall prepare himself to the battle?'

But Mr Timothy might well have gone on and given the next verse from this Pauline epistle (1 Corinthians 9): 'except you utter . . . plain speech, how shall it be known what is said? For you will be speaking into the air'.

Self-evidently, it is the BBC's first responsibility to ensure that it 'be known what is said', and it is only to this end (and not, for instance, for the sake of language standards *per se*) that the duty to 'uphold the standards of spoken English' arises. When one reflects on the range of listeners and viewers that are to be addressed, themselves observing a range of language standards of which pitifully little is known, the perceived 'duty' becomes as bewildering as it does onerous. When one further reflects on the amount of broadcasting throughout which the duty is to be maintained (in 1979 the BBC operated for over 420 hours a day in the UK services alone), it may well seem that the magnitude of the task puts it beyond the possibility of fulfilment.

To what extent a single set of standards is applicable to all services and all types of programme has long been a vexed question, but of one thing we can be quite certain: it is only in the most general terms that any such single set of standards could be imposed on all who come before microphone and camera. In this respect the analogies all too freely drawn between broadcasting authorities and the press are grossly false. The *Daily Mirror* and *The Times* can decide upon a 'house style' to a fair degree of detail and then impose it both upon their own staff and (through the diligent editing which the leisure of even the frenetic daily press permits) upon invited contributions from outside. Whether or not, in so doing, the press 'upholds the standards of English' — let alone feels 'a clear duty' about it — is of course another matter. My point is that the press undoubtedly has the means in a way and to a degree denied to broadcasting.

In the early days of the medium, when everything transmitted was scripted, the analogy was close enough. Only in pronunciation could the broadcaster have gone his own way and it was in this area that the Advisory Committee on Spoken English operated from 1926 to ensure that he did not — at least if he was one of the BBC's own broadcasting staff. Not that the preventive measures needed to be severe. Recruits to the young BBC were from the same educational (and social) background as those entering the law, medicine, the top branches of the press and civil service. They therefore 'spoke' (that is, pronounced) English in broadly the same way as their fellows in these professions — the 'Received Pronunciation' associated with the public schools and indeed with public pronouncements, whether from the Crown, the pulpit, the bench, or the ('legit') stage. All that the Advisory Committee felt it necessary to do was try to ensure consistency and to arbitrate in those cases where variation occurred within Received Pronunciation.[3] In so far, therefore, as 'BBC English' was not a misnomer (the BBC merely coming to be the chief medium in which the public at large encountered RP), it was for the most part only a mildly engineered and regularised selection from the already existing dominant variety of English used in the leading professions.

But of course even this modest degree of direction could be imposed only on the BBC's own microphone staff. There could never be any question of making this form of pronunciation the only English heard on the air: talks, short stories, drama and other entertainment from the earliest days were heard in a variety of regional and social accents, though of course care was taken (and while everything was scripted this was particularly easy) to control language presentation in a wider sense: the avoidance of coarseness, blasphemy and the like.

It would be fair to say, indeed, that it was in these far more pervasive areas of language — content, tone, style — that the image of a BBC manner grew up, and this came to be associated with, identified with, even determined by the cut-glass RP accents of announcers — 'BBC English': first as a *façon de parler*, then perhaps as a *façon de penser*. It was certainly convenient to have so easily referable a stick to beat the BBC with — as early as 1926:

> The BBC are determined to secure some uniformity of the English language as used in their studios . . . Now, so long as the BBC restrict their efforts to teaching announcers how to pronounce simple Scottish place-names all will be well; but when it comes to standardising the pronunciation of our whole mother-tongue we protest . . . There is a danger of 'BBC English' becoming a sort of criterion. (*Glasgow Evening Citizen*, 21 July 1926)

Evidence of the BBC's embarrassment is not difficult to find. Protestations of innocently limited objectives stretch into the 1970s from the mid-1920s when they were definitively uttered by John Reith himself: 'There has been no attempt to establish a uniform spoken language' — it was merely 'desirable to adopt uniformity . . . of pronunciation to be observed by announcers'.[4]

But there can be no question that the dominant role of RP within the BBC has been given an importance over the years that is out of all proportion to its relevance in the whole context of the BBC's communicative performance. In any case, the story has been so excellently told by Gerhard Leitner[5] that I may be forgiven for concentrating here on other aspects.

Reference has already been made to 'house style', and although — in relation to print — we think of this primarily in terms of language in its narrowest respects (spelling, for instance), it involves presentation rather widely. In the daily and weekly press, it concerns vocabulary choice, sentence length and other aspects of language, as well as column width, design of headlines and subheadings, typeface, use of pictures and their relation to text, and numerous other matters. After instructing his colleagues to be sparing in the use of 'crossheads' to break up and enliven copy, Waterhouse goes on:

> The standard Mirror crosshead consists of one word, usually of no

more than seven or eight characters . . . Abstract nouns that
relate to behaviour (*Sorrow, Theft, Attack*) are better than abstract
nouns that don't (*Role, Magic, Nights*) and infinitely better than
most concrete nouns (*Table, Coach, Lamp*). But verbs or adjectives
may be better still. *Stole* is better than *Theft*, night lawyers
allowing, and *Hot* is better than *Heat*.[6]

Not only is style by no means limited to features of language
(though these will remain my concern here) but equally no non-
linguistic aspect of style in the media can be without reference to
linguistic aspects. The *Daily Mirror*'s choice of racy stories and girlie
pictures is inevitably matched by such choices in language as we
have just seen being specified. So too it is to be expected that Dave
Lee Travis will match his comments to the style of music he
introduces on Radio 1 as radically as Colin Doran adapts himself to
introducing a choral mass on Radio 3. Nor has the BBC ever been
'monotone': the same announcer in the 1930s (Stuart Hibberd)
could permit himself a wide range between the sobriety appropriate
for announcing the death of a king and the relative heartiness of
introducing *Saturday Night Music Hall*.[7] And whatever jokes we now
make about announcers of old, dress-constrained despite their
invisibility, we must recognise that the sartorial elegance of Angela
Rippon or Kenneth Kendall before the camera today is equally an
inalienable part of the communicative style.

But style is more than a matter of 'house' (*Mirror* and *The Times*,
Radio 1 and Radio 3): it is also a matter of *medium* and *posture*. We do
not speak as we write. We choose clothes and speech for an interview
with a potential employer other than for a pub crawl with friends.[8]
And when we write to a person we do not know, we would be wise to
appreciate that we cannot automatically depend on his complete
understanding, let alone his co-operative sympathy. When there is a
shared field of discourse (e.g. psychology or law), we can of course
avoid some of the more obvious pitfalls of medium and posture by
writing within the conventions established in the field concerned: in
other words, by deliberately suppressing originality and as many
traces of our personality as possible.

When we find ourselves writing for a number of different
unknown people, of unknown professional interests and personal
tastes, the difficulties of course increase exponentially. They became
acute with the 'Gutenberg revolution', and William Caxton showed
his awareness of them five hundred years ago in a well-known

passage from the Prologue to the *Eneydos*. With book production no longer a matter of supplying one known customer with a known taste in manuscript style, it was necessary to effect some kind of 'meane', as Caxton called it, but with small possibility of avoiding every feature of language likely to displease someone or other. 'Fain would I satisfy every man', he wrote, but knew it was impossible 'because of diversity . . . of language'.

Analogous problems, but still more acute, confronted thirty-three-year-old John Reith in 1922 when he contemplated general management of the British Broadcasting Company. In opting (unsurprisingly) for a linguistic uniformity based (just as unsurprisingly) on what was perceived as the 'Best English' of the capital, Reith and his colleagues were in part merely following the reasoning of Caxton: the selection of a language form that would be understood and tolerated most widely. And despite the perennial objections to which I have referred, this has never been seriously challenged — at any rate so far as pronunciation is concerned, and indeed views like the following have been fairly generally expressed:

> For good or ill, what may be termed Southern English is understood more clearly over a greater area than even a slightly localized form of speech. Northcountry accent is not at all understood well in remote districts such as Devonshire. (*Yorkshire Observer*, 25 January 1943)

We may of course question this emphasis on comprehensibility: dialect-speaking comedians seem to have been understood across dialect boundaries without difficulty, and it is much more likely that the point most favouring 'Southern English' was its acceptability as the voice of prestige and authority. And indeed it seemed to Lloyd James that accents other than RP had lost their potential authority precisely through association with buffoonery — a process that has been going on for hundreds of years, as we see from the *Reeve's Tale*, let alone *Henry IV* and *Pickwick*:

> You mustn't blame the BBC for killing dialect. The Lancashire comedian has killed the Lancashire dialect, and made Lancashire for ever afterwards impossible for the production of Shakespeare.
>
> (*The Listener*, 2 March 1935)

But Reith's BBC had a further motive: to see its role not just in terms of entertainment, or even of information, but of improvement. The public was to be offered something better than it might think it liked — and the models of good taste ranged from the quality of jokes through the quality of music to the quality of language itself.[9] And many outside the BBC became convinced that the new access to a cultivated voice and way of talking would indeed bring about widespread imitation: a girl 'may encourage her young man to make pleasant sounds, as she stimulates him to wear more acceptable clothes'.[10] Together with the careful scrutiny of scripts (with these objectives very much in view), it was perhaps the self-consciously 'uplifting' goal of the BBC that contributed more than anything else to a certain turgidity, some pomposity of style that even today — after the traumatic 1960s and Carleton Greene — is often felt to mark the BBC (as distinct, for example, from ITV).

There was a related but separate problem for radio in the matter of *posture*. Limited analogies again occur with print. When a writer knows (or hopes) that he is going to be read by many, does he address them as intimate friends, respected strangers, avid pupils? As dependants, as superiors? They may include all of these but it is not easy to adopt a tone that is equally appropriate to them. And should he address them en masse ('Dear Brethren'), or pretend that he is writing to an individual ('Gentle Reader')?

There is abundant evidence that, with all the very real ambitions to reach out to and 'improve' the least affluent and the least privileged, the BBC addressed itself predominantly to the middle class — the people, after all, with whom the BBC staff could most realistically identify. C. A. Lewis, Reith's deputy organiser of programmes, listing in the *BBC Handbook 1928* the factors that distracted listeners' attention, included the maid entering with coffee. Though the sights seem to have been drastically lowered in recent years, radio and television are still unable to focus upon particular consumer groups of predictable economic standing or political orientation (as can writers for the daily press)[11] and so vaguely aim at a 'middle range'.[12]

And within this middle range, the principle was early established of pretended address to an individual person, isolated by his headphones or — later — within earshot of a 'loudspeaker', in a frequently darkened drawing-room. A note from the Artistic Director in July 1924[13] reads:

The mental attitude that you are performing to a vast unseen audience is, I feel, the wrong one to adopt. It is not mob psychology for which you have to cater but the psychology of the individual.

The stylistic correlates of this in personal warmth and directness seem to have worked in some types of programme (A. J. Alan, for example) better than with others, such as the news. But in any case the format of some programmes demanded that the individual be made to feel part of a large listening community — sometimes a worldwide one. Laurence Gilliam's Christmas Day 'hook-up' of 1939 contained such gestures as the following:

London calling[14] . . . across the wild Atlantic . . . to the great cities and white prairies of Canada, across the North and South Pacific . . . London calling across the oceans of the world.

'The style', as Black says[15] 'seems high-flown now, but it didn't then' — a significant comment from so informed an observer in that it draws attention both to the changed style and posture of the BBC today (still able to walk with kings, but adding a lot more of the common touch), and to the corresponding change in our attitudes and tastes as listeners.

In discussing medium earlier, our focus was upon the selection of a form of English suitable to a mass listening audience. But of course 'medium' in the broader sense (radio as distinct from print, video as distinct from audio) is bound to demand and may additionally engender medium-specific conventions of presentation with their own linguistic correlates. To take an obvious point: the eye alone can see what is the beginning and what is the ending of a newspaper article; on radio (and to a lesser extent on television), beginnings and endings must be made orally explicit: 'This is the National Programme. Here is the weather forecast . . . ' 'BBC Radio Four. A Book at Bedtime . . . ' 'And here we are, back in the Royal Festival Hall'. As can be seen from these examples, the conventions lead to the establishment of formulae, some of which (especially those most neutral in tone) may remain in currency for long periods while others are flexibly responsive to changes in general style with the passing of time, or to differences related to types of broadcast. Rohdenburg discusses the interesting range from 'And that concludes this edition . . . ' to 'And that, I'm afraid, is about all we've time for' or 'Well, that winds up our First Sports Forum'.[16] Even the use of demonstratives is formulaic and Rohdenburg quotes a letter from the BBC in 1970 explaining that

> 'And this brings to an end . . . ' would hardly ever be used unless 'this' was still going on while the announcer was speaking. Normally, 'that' refers to an item which has just ended.

Endemic, of course, in programme announcements, medium-specific formulae and style clichés seem otherwise to be most noticeable in the presentation of news, where their development over the years (for example, in providing verbal linkage between news items, another feature scarcely known in the printed press) has shown dramatic change and where indeed the entire style of presentation has shifted most radically. This is in part inevitable since responsibility itself for the news changed fundamentally from the early days in which the BBC merely gave out what the agencies offered (and duly credited them with the copyright) to the establishment of the BBC's own news investigation service. Less inevitably, the role of presenter changed too. At first a totally impersonal and unidentified voice (fittingly enough for material 'by' agencies outside the BBC and fittingly enough for the impersonal language style of this material), later with self-credited voices ('Here is the news and this is X reading it'),[17] later still to the increasing suggestion that the presenter is *telling* us the news and not just reading it. This is hinted at in the pen seen in the presenter's hand for some news presentations — suggesting that the presenter has prepared his own notes — and more than hinted at in others by the use of a lens-located 'autocue' to disguise the fact that the presenter is reading the material (in sharp contrast to the equally conventional insistence in some other countries that the news be given greater authority than the presenter's by ensuring that he is *seen* to be reading a formal script). And Angela Rippon's terminal formula is 'That's it from me', a style that is a far cry not only from the linguistic formality but from the disjoined responsibility of 'That is the end of the news'.

Since the direction of stylistic change in handling the news seems to be fully congruent with — indeed conveniently representative of — stylistic change in the BBC's output as a whole, it may be useful to compare two broadcasts more than thirty years apart. In both cases, the text represents an attempt to reconstruct the script based solely on a transcription of the version as heard over the air and nothing is known about the extent (doubtless very little, if at all, in the first case) to which the presenters departed from the script in front of them.[18]

1. The first is a news broadcast of 5 February 1938, read (anonymously) by Mr Alvar Lidell:

Here is the third news. Copyright reserved.
The changes in Germany in the control of Armed Forces and of foreign policy fill columns in the international press today. The French papers, as well as the German and Italian, are agreed on one point: that the changes mean a very large extension of the control of the Armed Forces 5 by the Nazi party. And this, needless to say, is enthusiastically welcomed in the German and Italian press. It causes grave misgiving in France. It is only necessary to quote a few sentences from one German paper to give an idea of the official reaction throughout the German press. The *Lokalanzeiger* says, 'The uniting of the supreme military leader- 10 ship in the Leader's own hands will undoubtedly accelerate the process of welding the Party and the Armed Forces together. The Party represented by its head, the Leader, and the Army represented by its Supreme Commander, also the Leader, have been knitted together in the person of Adolf Hitler. How ridiculous therefore must the silly talk in the foreign 15 press appear about disharmonies and alleged differences of political outlook'. Signor Mussolini has sent a telegram of congratulation to Herr Hitler expressing great satisfaction at his assuming the effective command of all the Armed Forces of Germany. Signor Mussolini says that this will strengthen the comradeship between the armed forces and the 20 regimes of Italy and Germany. Herr Hitler, in his reply, says he will consider his task to strengthen further the political and ideological relations which already exist between Germany and Italy. Signor Mussolini has also sent telegrams of congratulation to Baron von Neurath on becoming head of the new secret Cabinet Council, to Herr von Ribbentrop 25 on becoming Foreign Minister, and to Field Marshal Göring on becoming Field Marshal Göring. The new Field Marshal is reported already to have taken the opportunity of wearing his new Field Marshal's uniform. He wore it today when he opened a private exhibition of the Academy of Arts in Berlin. The reactions in France to the changes may be summed up by a 30 quotation from *Le Journal*. 'Control of the army', it says, 'henceforth becomes entirely dependent on the Nazi party which is now supreme and undis undisputed master and the great and only victor of the days of crisis. Generals who have thought they could exercise influence, even though indirectly on the policy of the Reich . . . who had only luke-warm faith 35 in the military worth of the new Italy, and who moreover found that the Spanish affair had already lasted too long, these generals are beaten by the Party, which imposes its ideas and which knows only one foreign policy: that of Herr Hitler. The appointment of Herr von Ribbentrop is more than abundant proof of this and gives a stinging denial to those who 40 proclaimed the Rome-Berlin axis is shaken.'

In Vienna, the German news has also caused misgiving, but hope is felt there that the new Cabinet Council may have a moderating influence on German foreign policy. There have been several rumours about the retired Commander in Chief of the Army, General von Fritsch, that he was or had been 45 under arrest and that he had been removed because of his relations with the French army command.

II. The second is a news broadcast, also on sound radio, of 3 January 1972, the 'upgrading' of the presenter made manifest not merely by his being named but by his being actually presented by an announcer:

Announcer: Eight o'clock on Monday, the third of January, and here's the news, from Brian Hudson.
Hudson: The headlines this morning: Northern Ireland: Troops battle with a crowd at a Belfast club. Malta: abuzz with rumour as a Libyan plane flies in with forty men. Vietnam: President Nixon says Hanoi must 5 negotiate or the Americans will keep a force there. A New York gang clean out the strong boxes of a Fifth Avenue hotel.
First, Northern Ireland, and a pitched battle early this morning at a social club in Belfast. Two civilians and one soldier were slightly hurt as a crowd of people barricaded inside fought to keep out 10 troops who'd gone to the club to check who was there. From Belfast, Chris Drake:
Drake: There were nearly two hundred men and women in the Saint Mary's Hall club, which is just off the York Road, in Cause Lane, when the army cordoned off the area and began their operation soon after ten o'clock 15 last night, then told the management they intended carrying out a check on all the people present, and within an hour seventy-four had left peacefully. The rest remained inside. They barricaded the doors and windows with billiard tables, chairs and other furniture, and refused to leave. It was a couple of hours later, when repeated appeals by the 20 army had failed, that men of the Second Fusiliers began trying to break the doors down. They were met by a barrage of bits of broken furniture, bottles, glasses, billiard balls and cues, and for half an hour the pitched battle continued . . .
Hudson: Next, Malta. About five hundred and fifty troops are now known to 25 be on stand-by in Britain in case they're needed to help in the evacuation from the island . . . Our defence correspondent understands there are no firm plans at present for flying any of the men out to Malta, but they will be needed there if the troops stationed on the island find themselves having to prepare for evacuation without the help of civilian 30 employees. Now, with details of the latest situation in Malta, our Commonwealth correspondent, Jim Biddulph:
Biddulph: The flood of rumours connected with the British withdrawal were given a massive boost here last night when a Hercules transport plane of the Libyan air force landed at the airport. It is said to have unloaded 35 about forty personnel plus cargo . . .

At about the same time as the second of these broadcasts, the BBC was conducting a fairly extensive investigation into the public reception of its news. A 'formal, serious, humourless and establishment image' was found to result in part from 'unnecessary complexity of language, and a stiffness and formality in presentation'.[19] If this verdict was applicable to picture-assisted news on BBC TV (and it is endorsed by the Glasgow Group's own findings),[20] how much more so must it have applied to such material as that exemplified above in the 1938 broadcast? Quite apart from the amount of time devoted to the item and the startlingly trivial degree of detail (Göring wearing his new uniform 'today when he opened a private exhibition of the Academy of Arts in Berlin'), the lexical and syntactic texture is essentially that of print, indeed of the *small* print found in the 'quality' newspapers of the day. This can be seen in comparing the style of the matrix material with that of the translated inserts from the German and French press. These are, if anything, livelier and more readily comprehensible to the ear than the embedding discourse prepared in the BBC itself for the ear alone: 'expressing great satisfaction at his assuming the effective command of all the Armed Forces of Germany', 'hope is felt there that the new Cabinet Council may have a moderating influence on German foreign policy'.

But whether we have translated quotation or BBC text, the whole is read by one single, cultured voice, the abstract, unimaginative, monotone dullness matched by a monotone, impersonal remoteness in the reading[21] with only one sign of human frailty as Lidell 'fluffs' the word *undisputed*. At the same time, we should note how rudimentary are the medium-determined conventions (virtually nothing beyond the opening formula, 'Here is the third news'), and how unlikely that listeners would have raised the kind of objections familiar in more recent times ('sloppy' colloquialism, media clichés and mannerisms). The vocal and the literate who liked the style of *The Times* would find little fault with the news on radio.

With all this, the 1972 example is in stark contrast. In so far as we are reminded of the press, it is now the *Mirror* rather than *The Times* ('abuzz with rumour', 'pitched battle'), and indeed a reminder of the press is inescapable. The device of press headlines has been adopted, with a metaphorical extension of the term itself and with imitation of the style and grammar concerned — notably in the use of the present tense ('troops battle', 'Nixon says'). Press journalism seems also to be influencing presentation in the device of sequential expansion. The few words on Northern Ireland in the 'headlines' are slightly expanded in lines 8–11, with significant lexical repetition for endorsement (*battle, club, crowd, troops*); the insert that follows from Belfast (lines 13 ff.) is not only a further expansion but is a full repetition of what we have already been told twice.

But clearly we are not offered a replica of popular press style as directly as the 1938 excerpt replicated the style of 'quality' papers. Broadcast news has adapted press devices to the needs of the specific medium and has developed others in addition. Headlines in a paper are not grouped at the beginning but are distributed along with the news items that they summarise; and they are generally briefer than those broadcast, as well as being stripped of grammatical devices like articles and auxiliaries.

The self-confidence of broadcasters in evolving their own stylistic strategies can be seen in the way headlines themselves involve the sequential expansion I have mentioned. A superordinate 'heading' in the form of a verbless clause ('Northern Ireland') is characteristically followed by a brief sentential 'headline' summarising the news item concerned: 'Troops battle with a crowd . . .' . A related and still more striking characteristic is the way in which such a superordinate verbless heading (usually a noun phrase) is then formally co-ordinated by *and* with the expansion concerned, even though no co-ordination in the grammatical sense is possible. This stylistic cliché occurs in line 8, and is a daily commonplace: 'The Olympic games and most athletes are determined to take part'.

The verbless clause (along with short, snappy sentences and the colloquial contractions like *here's* that were once conspicuously absent from news reading) contributes prominently to the new free-wheeling breezy style of presentation. 'Eight o'clock on Monday.' 'The headlines this morning.' 'Next, Malta.' It is perhaps especially notable in the formulae used to introduce inserts, such formulae themselves characterised by preposed adverbials: 'From Belfast, Chris Drake'. 'With details of the latest situation . . . Jim Biddulph.' Before this type of insert became so common, far more explicit and deliberate switching was used: 'Now we go over to our X correspondent in Y' (with nonetheless a medium-specific metaphor in *go over*).

These presentational devices are, of course, interactive. The inserts, obviously unnecessary in any strict sense, are believed to convey immediacy and authenticity. But immediacy also demands a certain colloquialism and an avoidance of the impression that time has been available to endow a careful, literary style. And if colloquialism is therefore a desideratum, a careful consistent pronunciation and elocution can no longer be. Given indeed the dominance of inserts from a variety of far-flung speakers who obviously cannot be subjected to detailed linguistic control, it would be disturbing if there were too obvious a stylistic contrast between these and the studio-based presenters. The same arguments reduce — to say the least — the need to insist on strict RP accents. As in the Germany of the 1930s, so in the UK of the 1980s, 'Rundfunksprache ist kein phonetisches Problem, sondern ein stilistisches'.[22]

I am not of course suggesting that all stylistic devices on radio and television are thus logically purposive. As with cliché in general, many of them result from lack of time and lack of care, as journalists take the easy well-worn path to provide a hurried ninety-second stretch of oral 'copy'. There is for example the overuse of the cleft sentence to provide little-wanted focus upon time adverbials, as in line 20: '*It was* a couple of hours later . . . *that* men . . . began . . .'

So also, in the six o'clock news of 13 October 1971, an insert by Tom Bostock: '*It was* early this morning *that* journalists . . . were taken . . . to the scene . . .'.

But in general the stylistic changes are both medium-determined and conscious. To a great extent they are deliberate responses to a pervasive democratisation in our society as a whole, a recognition that 'broadcasting must be part of the democratic tree and all broadcasters must realise that they are sitting on one of its branches'.[23] Already, in the 1960s, Hugh Carleton Greene was pointing out that a proper relationship between broadcasters and the public 'cannot exist if the language in which they are talking, and the assumptions they are making, seem to be too remote from the language and assumptions of the audience and of the times in which they are communicating'.[24]

But the problems here are legion. The audience must inevitably talk a wide range of language, the details of which are little known to linguists let alone to BBC production staff. Nor are the audience's assumptions readily known: they have themselves to be assumed, with a corresponding (if fairly safe) assumption that the assumptions are spectrally ranging. What will be seen in some sectors of the population as a timidly belated response to changes in thresholds, tolerances, sensibilities will be resented by other sectors as enforcing an unacceptable pace of change — and in directions that are equally resented. For many people, the BBC's recently acquired air of derring-do seems as unrepresentatively *dirigiste* as the Reithian concept of giving audiences 'what they ought to want' — though it is precisely against the remnants of such a policy that the new style has been directed.

The simple polarity of 'hieratic' and 'demotic' has thus only limited application in a complex society such as our own. The BBC's hieratic style of fifty years ago was the easier for broadcasters to use since — with their education and background[25] — it was fairly natural for them and hence close to a demotic. But the new demotic stance in Broadcasting House and Television Centre is only in the most general terms closer to the speech perception and performance of the population at large — and hence it can be widely received as a quasi-hieratic. The result has been to attract attacks from different sections of the population on quite different aspects of presentational style.

We have had, for instance, predictable tirades against what is seen as the new sloppiness ('this strata', 'infer' for 'imply', and the like). There was deemed to be such 'wide public concern about the standard of spoken English on the BBC' in 1979 that Mr Aubrey Singer invited a month's surveillance of output. In the event, the trio of observers found little enough to upset them and were equally unimpressed by the evidence of wide public concern or the sources of complaint: 'all the letters were written by middle-aged or by elderly people'.[26] Although this point does not of itself invalidate the complaints (even the most youthful members of a society are sometimes wrong), the experience of the observers matches that of the Annan Committee who received rather few protests about 'poor English'.

More serious has been the way in which people have felt alienated by the tones of easy sophistication that have accompanied the trend to informality. Such people have included the black and brown immigrants who can feel excluded at best and — worse — can suspect that they are being slighted. And they have included large numbers of the working and lower middle class who — whatever their own standards are in private talk — are easily offended by breaches of linguistic convention in the media (a point significantly respected by even the most scandal-oriented sections of the public press). 'Some are outraged by what to them are blasphemous expletives; others by sexual or scatological words'.[27] Standards in these matters are not nearly as volatile as the avant-garde would like to think, but they are nonetheless notoriously variable at any moment within a given society.[28] It is clear that the major media, printed and broadcast alike, need to tread warily and to exercise considerable self-censorship. And indeed they do. The danger of libel and other legal infringements have constantly to be watched. Political sensitivities demand in-house conferences to decide whether a blood-letting has involved 'terrorists' or 'nationalists' or 'freedom fighters'. Broadcasting staff must carefully interpret the law of the land in refraining from language suggestive of racial prejudice: there should be no 'welshing'. They must, indeed, go beyond the mere law in being alert to social sensibilities, respecting such movements as 'gay lib', 'women's lib' and of course religious beliefs, beyond the call of statute. As Robert Robinson has wisely said, 'The broadcaster has . . . an obligation to tread a delicate path — not under any moral obligation, but simple good manners enjoin it'. But more than good manners are involved. It takes the sharpened insights of the experienced communicator to acquire a full respect for the linguistic instrument by which man both releases his fancy and reflects his mythologies.

Thus when our society's vanguard is looking for 'inclusionary policies', broadcasters are wise to speak rather of 'the average *person*' than of 'the *man* in the street'—just as they are wise to recognise that 'claiming responsibility' with respect to IRA activity has positive and victorious overtones. This is the sort of issue that is on the agenda for the weekly meetings, for example, of the BBC's News and Current Affairs personnel, and they are among the issues that are clearly set forth for the newsmen of radio in the 70-page booklet, *BBC News Guide*. This is not, of course, to say that the existence of the 'style sheet' mentality is always advantageous. It is said that the BBC 'cocked up the assassination of President Kennedy' because it could not be readily decided whether this required the procedure for a head of state's death 'or whether it was just a crime'.[29]

But although such controls exist, they are limited in extent and they are, so to say, 'defensive': they aim at protecting the BBC's interest in one way or another (whether avoiding legal action or a listener's complaint or a loss of audience). The question arises whether controls might (i) have a wider purview, and (ii) have more outward-looking goals, perhaps to 'purify the dialect of the tribe' if not actually return to concepts of wholesale 'cultural therapy'.

The answer to (i) is in my view 'yes'. I have long regretted (though understanding the evolutionary reasons) that, alone among the linguistic performance factors, pronunciation was given such importance as to justify a special unit to provide in-house guidance. There seems in fact to have been a drastic narrowing of the concept Reith enunciated to his new-born 'Advisory Committee on Spoken English' in June 1926, that it should help the BBC 'to stem modern tendencies to inaccurate and slurred speech' — which certainly does not suggest a restriction to issues of 'Received Pronunciation'. Subsequently, one member of the Committee, Logan Pearsall Smith, kept returning to the need to tackle broader linguistic issues and in an undated memorandum we find him urging that they take into 'consideration not only the pronunciation but the choice and the formation of words'.[30] He seems to have been unsuccessful.

After being a member of the committee responsible for appointing a new head of the Pronunciation Unit in the summer of 1978, and hence having had an opportunity to consider the present responsibilities of the Unit (largely reduced, with the severely diminished insistence on RP, to advising on the pronunciation of names, British and foreign), I wrote to BBC management suggesting 'a broader-based unit'. Since there was now strong evidence that the public in this country (and still more abroad[31]) expected 'the BBC to represent and reflect the best standards of current English' and since linguistic scholarship has furnished us with far sounder reference works on English lexicon, grammar and sociolinguistic factors in usage as a whole than were available fifty years ago, I argued that there was a good case for providing production departments with far-reaching guidelines on language and style. These guidelines would emphasise the falsity of outmoded beliefs in a single, invariant 'standard' in language as in culture at large. Catholicity, authenticity and flexibility are superior watchwords, and I have been impressed in discussions with trainee producers at the readiness to appreciate this.

If my answer to (i) is 'yes', it is because I believe in the positive influence of broadcasting services on the extended response to — and probably on the active use of — the language. It is not easy to demonstrate the truth of this and in reaction to early naïveties on this subject (which looked, essentially, for 'social climbing' reactions in the spread of class accents)[32] it has become fashionable to deny influence entirely — on linguistic as on other aspects of behaviour.

But the Annan Committee reviewed the issue in some detail and seemed to conclude (with Lord Clark) that television — for example — 'had enormously widened people's horizons; it had increased their knowledge of the world and of nature, and even whetted their appetites for art and ideas',[33] just as no one has seriously questioned that radio in the Reith era had extended the public's taste in music. None of this can be true without a corresponding extension in the public's sensitivity to and knowledge of language. And Fishman has stoutly reasserted the media's influence in respect of language standards.[34]

But a 'yes' answer to (i) would still not require a 'yes' answer to (ii), affirming that broadcasting authorities have an actual responsibility to raise the public's standards, whether in language or in anything else. It is much easier in this instance to muster arguments in favour of a negative answer. The strongest and the most obvious is that the more overt and active such a therapeutic policy, the greater would be the resistance not only from listeners and viewers but from the programme and production staff within broadcasting. The BBC could best fulfil a role of influencing for good by providing — within such obvious limits as legal constraint — free rein to its creative staff. *Preaching* what is believed to be best in language, art and culture as a whole is no job for broadcasting authorities: it is enough that they be free to *reflect* the best: the realistic, plural best.

NOTES

1. For ready assistance in assembling material for this paper, I am grateful to Richard Hewlett and several other officers of the BBC, particularly those working in sound and written archives.
2. R. W. Burchfield, D. Donoghue and A. Timothy, *The Quality of Spoken English on BBC Radio* (BBC, London, 1979).
3. The consequent neglect of lexical and grammatical aspects of presentation seriously contributed to the BBC's reputation for using 'difficult' language, and I return to this point below.
4. J. Reith, *Broadcast English*, I (BBC Publication, 1928).
5. Especially G. Leitner, *BBC English und der BBC: Geschichte und Soziolinguistische Interpretation des Sprachgebrauchs in einem Massenmedium, Linguistische Berichte,* Papier 60 (Braunschweig), 1979, and also ' "BBC English" and "Deutsche Rundfunksprache": A Comparative and Historical Analysis of the Language of Radio', *International Journal of the Sociology of Language* (1980).
6. K. Waterhouse, *Daily Mirror Style* (Mirror Group, London, 1979).
7. Something of this kind was the subject of an internal BBC memorandum of

1936 ('one voice . . . many styles'), referred to in T. Burns, *The BBC: Public Institution and Private World* (Macmillan, London, 1977), p. 26.

8. R. Quirk, S. Greenbaum, G. Leech and J. Svartvik, *A Grammar of Contemporary English* (Longman, London, 1972), pp. 15ff.

9. Compare Burns, op. cit., p. 36.

10. T. H. Pear, *Voice and Personality* (Chapman and Hall, London, 1931).

11. Though 'generic programming' from the late sixties went some way to 'solving' this problem — and creating new ones: cf. Home Office: *Report of the Committee on the Future of Broadcasting*, Chairman, Lord Annan, Cmnd. 6753 (HMSO, London, 1977).

12. Glasgow University Media Group, *Bad News* (Routledge and Kegan Paul, London, 1976).

13. Compare Leitner (1979), op. cit., p. 34.

14. A formula still remembered in the title of the monthly magazine of the World Service.

15. P. Black, *The Biggest Aspidistra in the World: a personal celebration of fifty years of the BBC* (BBC Publications, London, 1972), p. 91.

16. G. Rohdenburg, 'Rundfunksendungsschlüsse im Englischen und Deutschen', *PAKS-Arbeitsbericht*, 7 (Stuttgart, 1973).

17. From 1940; this is usually said to result from wartime security needs, but cf. Black, op. cit. p. 94.

18. Both transcriptions are reproduced by kind permission of the British Broadcasting Corporation.

19. Glasgow Media Group, op. cit., pp. 5f.

20. Ibid., p. 27.

21. Compare D. Crystal, *The English Tone of Voice* (Edward Arnold, London, 1975), p. 91.

22. Leitner (1980), op. cit., p. 22.

23. S. Hearst, 'Has "Public Service Broadcasting" a Future?', *Encounter*, May 1979, p. 14.

24. Quoted in Burns, op. cit., p. 152.

25. Burns, op. cit., p. 98ff.

26. Burchfield *et al.*, op. cit., p. 8.

27. Annan, op. cit., p. 258.

28. Compare R. Quirk, 'Sound Barriers and *Gangbangsprache*', in C. Ricks and L. Michaels, (eds) *The State of the Language* (University of California Press, London, 1979).

29. Glasgow Media Group, op. cit., p. 80.

30. I am endebted to Professor David Abercrombie for this reference.

31. The BBC's responsibility for ensuring a good standard of English in its World Service (especially in view of the world importance of English: cf. B. H. Jernudd and W. D. Shaw, *World Maps of Uses of English and Other Languages of Wider Communication* (East-West Center, Honolulu, 1979, mimeo), raises issues that must regretfully be excluded from the scope of this paper.

32. 'Millions of listeners will be influenced by the way announcers speak' (*The Star*, 16 January 1940). Cf. also Pear, op. cit. pp. 82ff. The advent of radio and then of the 'talkies' gave rise to much public discussion of voice and pronunciation—in much the same way as the advent of printing was followed by numerous treatises on orthography.

33. Annan, op. cit. p. 24, and cf. also P. H. Newby, *Radio, Television and the Arts* (BBC, London, 1976).

34. J. Fishman, 'The Sociology of Language', in T. Sebeok, *Current Trends in Linguistics*, vol. 12 (Mouton, The Hague, 1974).

7 Karl Deutsch

Choice can be a privilege, an opportunity, a fundamental right, a risk or a burden. But what do we mean by the concept?

By subjective choice I mean a choice between two or more anticipated courses of action or behaviour. By objective choice I mean a decision among two or more courses of behaviour with different consequences, short-run or long-run, foreseen or unforeseen. When a dog runs out into the street in front of a moving car and the driver does not step on the brake he may have decided about the fate of the dog whether he was aware of it or not. Inaction may be no less decisive than action.

We think most often of choice as something exercised by an individual, perhaps as a consumer or in other matters of his personal life. The greater his latitude of decision, the greater is the range of his freedom.

But there is also a range of choices for a society as a whole. Society may choose collectively, usually through some political procedure, whether to run its economic affairs by the methods of the marketplace, or by government regulation of private enterprise, or by central planning, or by some mixture of all these. It may choose, often by more informal methods, whether to be more strict or more permissive in the upbringing of its young, but this too is a choice which is not entirely in the hands of just the parents of each child alone.

Individuals also may choose, within limits, to which society they wish to belong, or what they want their community to be like. Conversely, society may try to choose what kinds of individuals it wishes to contain, perhaps by regulating immigration or by trying to influence through education the skills and character of the next generation.

Choices can go wrong, even from the viewpoint of the values held by those people who made them. Or the fear that they could go wrong in this manner may impose a burden of anxiety and anticipated guilt upon those who are to choose. In situations that appear particularly obscure and dangerous the burden of choice may overtake an individual's capacity for choosing and he or she may find that burden well nigh intolerable. Here we find the well-known cases of German soldiers who according to an old saying disliked 'being forced to command' and enjoyed 'being permitted to obey'.

In general the felt burden of choice is inversely related to the capacities of the individual who has to choose. Psychological studies in the United States army at the time of the Second World War reported that soldiers who had had no more than primary education became anxious and resentful when given indoctrination lectures containing arguments for and against a proposed course of action; soldiers with at least some college education, on the contrary, like lectures of this type. Lectures giving only one side of the argument were preferred by soldiers with only a grade-school education, but resented by the even partially college-educated ones. Tests of the retention of the subject matter taught in these lectures, both shortly after the sessions and several weeks later, show the same contrasts between these two categories of soldiers. Sociological studies of what has been called 'the authoritarianism of the poor' point in the same direction, but it is possible that the presence or absence of knowledge and relevant memories, rather than poverty, may be the decisive factor. If one considers that entire nations have progressed during the twentieth century from illiteracy to an average level of grade-school education, and other nations have progressed from an average of grade-school level to an average of secondary education and may now be on their way to an average and median corresponding to the British matriculation or the junior college in the United States, the demand for greater freedom of choice among these populations may well be increasing in the future—even if the authoritarian dictatorial governments of some of these countries had no such intention.

Communications systems as instruments of choice

If choice is not to be made blindly, it requires information which must be communicated to the decision-making individual or group. Beyond this, the communications system of a society has general functions. It transmits information and permits cognition, co-ordination and control, that is to say the steering and self-steering of large groups of human beings.

In most large societies several kinds of communications systems exist side by side. Economic communication and information may be transmitted by markets. Families, cultures and systems of social status may transmit other kinds of communication. Governments are also systems of communication through their legislative, executive and judicial branches; and there is a cognitive subsystem of society carried on largely through the subsystems of education, science and research and the mass media, including, notably, broadcasting, both in its radio and television form. In some sense these cognitive subsystems, taken together, do have a kind of quasi-governmental power, particularly in a democracy, as was demonstrated in the United States at the time of President Nixon's misfortunes in the Watergate affair.

In analysing a major communications system we may ask more generally what functions it must perform in order to operate and what particular capabilities and vulnerabilities may result from them.

A simple model of a communications system

Any major communications system must take in information through its receptors, preferably through a plurality of channels. It must then select some of this information according to some criteria of selection, by some filtering process, and it may amplify some of the information thus selected. It has to store this information in memory and recall from memory some information stored there earlier, combining it with some of the currently incoming information for a decision. If a communications system can do this, its behaviour cannot be wholly predicted even from a complete knowledge of its intake and output; it has some internal combinatorial freedom and thus some genuine autonomy. The recalled information may include some stable elements about a goal state in relation to the outside world, at which the system's internal disequilibrium will be reduced. If so, we are in the presence of a goal-seeking system, provided its effectors permit it to act in an appropriate manner.

More complex combinatorial processes may occur in regard to the information within the memory itself. Stored patterns of information may be dissociated; we may remember wings separately from a bird. Dissociated pieces of information may then be recombined; we may imagine wings attached to a human body and think of human flight well before the first aeroplane. Such dissociations and recombinations permit genuine *creativity* and *novelty*, and they may lead to *initiative* when applied to effector output and behaviour. When applied to the system's internal goal-setting processes, such novelty may turn it into a goal-changing system.

In any case, information from memory, whether simply recalled or transformed by recombination, is combined with currently incoming information for a decision which in turn communicates an instruction to the effectors of the system and perhaps also to a feedback of information to the memory so that the system may remember what it tried to do, or what it is still trying to do. In this case we may think of the action programme to which it is committed as its *intention*.

The effector output itself, in so far as it has taken place is the action of the system. A self-steering system then requires a feedback of information about the external results of this action, and perhaps also a feedback of the internal results of this same action upon some parts of the system itself. From this feedback information a new cycle of communication and decision can be started, again in combination with information that is currently coming in. If the sequence of cycles functions correctly, the system may be able to approach or maintain a goal state in which its internal dis-equilibrium is at some relative minimum. The process may, however, break down or go wrong at any stage, though some stages are more vulnerable than others.

More complex systems may derive highly abbreviated secondary symbols from the primary messages moving through the system, and they may use these greatly shortened 'messages about messages' for simultaneous inspection and decision, with appropriate channels of communication from this secondary decision centre from and to the various parts of the system. In this manner the system can fulfil some of the functions of *consciousness* of its own behaviour. Flow charts in directors' offices or plotting-rooms at aircraft operation centres are examples. Finally the system, if it has appropriate channels, may make decisions to reset its filters for screening out certain kinds of external information. Certain information that came in prior to this partial closing of the filters could still enter into the making of a decision but now that the decision has 'hardened' later information can no longer change the course of action. In this manner predecision messages will tend to prevail over post-decision ones. This process resembles what we individually experience as *will*. Some exercise of will is necessary for individuals, groups and states in order to get any course of action completed. But it is not without cost for will is the capacity not to learn.

It may be noticed that in a complex communications system of this type there is no single locus of supreme authority. Even the decisions at the level of the 'big board' or the operations room may be marred by inadequate information, or by failure to receive the appropriate data from memory, or by lack of sufficient control over the effector systems, or by inadequate feedback of information of the results of what has been done thus far.

If one applies this primitive model to a broadcasting system certain stages in the information-processing sequences stand out. The system's performance will depend in part on the richness and diversity of the intake of information which its reporters, micro-phones and cameras pick up. It may depend crucially upon the selection of the information chosen for transmission and perhaps on the amplification or exaggeration of the items selected. Perform-ance may further depend on the richness and appropriateness of information recalled from the memories, files and records of the system, as well as from the personal memories of its staff, and it may also depend on:

(1) Context: (i) what is the message about? Jocular or serious, love letter or business proposition? (ii) how important is it because of its source or its topic? (iii) what are the interests and intentions of the sender?

(2) Content: What does it say?

(3) Substantive value relevance (Freud's Id or Leisure Principle): what does it matter to anything I care for?

(4) Truth (Freud's Reality Principle): (i) does it seem true in itself? (ii) is it consonant with what else I know? How does it fit into my image of the world?

(5) Moral relevance (Freud's Superego): is it legitimate?

(6) Relevance to self-image (Freud's Ego): what will it do to my self-respect and to the respect others have for me?

(7) Action relevance: what do I have to do about it and with what expectable results?

These seemingly simple questions can also be given more complex-sounding names. The first two questions are associated with what we usually call *semantics* in the narrower sense. The next four deal largely with the interplay of conscious and unconscious *emotions* that can be listed under four headings paralleling those used by the psychiatrist Sigmund Freud in his otherwise more complex model of the individual human psyche. The last question — number seven — parallels what is often called pragmatics — the practical implications and consequences of the message. Together, these seven steps constitute a primitive outline of the process of interpretation, which is sometimes studied in the field of *hermeneutics*.

It should be noted that the answers to these seven questions may be different for each receiver in accordance with what he knows, what he values, what he has learnt and what he feels. It should also be noted that the same seven questions may have different answers for the sender from whom the message originated than they had for the receiver who gets it. If so, prodigious misunderstandings may result. If the receiver sends a message in return, a fruitful dialogue may result, if the two partners have memories sufficiently attuned to each other, that is, sufficiently similar to permit understanding and sufficiently different to sustain interest. If these conditions are absent, the dialogue may quickly cease or may produce a concatenation of misunderstandings and perhaps end in frustration, anxiety and rage.

Some key tasks of the broadcasting system today

Choice is one of the values a broadcasting system should offer to its users. But it is not the only value and some other tasks may be more fundamental.

Three tasks are basic: to preserve and strengthen the identity, autonomy and integration of the nation, state and community whom this broadcasting system serves.

By *identity* is meant the applicability of memory. When they no longer can apply their own memories to themselves, individuals with amnesia or groups in dissolution have lost their inner identity; when others can no longer apply their memories to them, they have lost their identity in the eyes of others.

Autonomy means the capacity for self-steering and self-direction; as set forth above, it is largely based on the use of memory.

Last but not least there is *integration*, that is, the coherence of a people so that what happens to some of them has predictable effects on others, and that they can do things together which no smaller group among them could — and which they want to do. For the individual, integration means a sense of belonging to the group, people or nation. It is what the social psychologist David McClelland called 'need for affiliation' and what Shirley Williams has spoken of as 'ligatures'.

Serving these three tasks sometimes can be accomplished at least in part in the form of entertainment but the importance of the service goes far beyond entertainment. In so far as the service is truly needed, broadcasting makes a major contribution to it; the importance of the service can hardly be measured in money. But can these tasks be performed? As pointed out earlier, the meaning of a message depends in large part upon the memories of those who receive it. The same broadcast might unite Orangemen but enrage Irish Catholics—or the other way around. What pleases Englishmen may not be equally pleasing to too many Scotsmen, as some of the BBC's audience surveys attest. To be meaningful *and* effective, messages must be adapted to the memories of the different audiences to whom they are addressed.

This leads us to a fourth major task of broadcasting: the *adaptation to the needs of people*. If people in different regions and groups — ethnic, regional, subcultural or social — all are to have their common identity, autonomy and integration strengthened, broadcasting must adapt to their particular and diverse needs. This may be particularly true for those relatively marginal regions and groups that may be crucial for the continuation of the whole.

Two images will illustrate this task. The first is a manipulative one. It is the image of the angler who always feeds enough line to the fish to keep him on the hook and does not let him get away. It is a policy of making enough concessions to the different needs and interests of each group while maintaining their links to the nation. The second image is an integrative one. It is the image of two people courting, falling in love and staying in love with each other. Since divorces became legal in most highly developed countries, most marriages have survived, but they had to be based on continuing consent. From Scotland to Quebec, something similar may be beginning to apply to the unity of large nations composed of a plurality of smaller peoples.

Another major task of adaptation will be adaptation to external needs. The problems of providing food for a world population that seems likely to double within the next forty years, to provide energy

and capital for an industrialising world, to protect the su.
peoples against the danger of major wars fought with wea₁
mass destruction — all this will require major efforts of
learning and adaptation. It cannot be done by preaching or do₍
or by the pretence that our present knowledge is wholly adequate
for this job and merely requires zeal and application. Rather it will
require us to think of knowledge as a matter of search, more than of
preaching, and here again the gradual, cumulative influence of
broadcasting could make a major difference.

Some particular issues

If there is any truth in the arguments thus far presented, they should
have implications for the financing of a broadcasting system. If one
of its major tasks is to promote social integration, its finances and
fees should be so arranged as to include, not exclude, marginal or
weaker social groups. Perhaps licence fees could be graded, so as to
make them cheaper in poorer regions and still cheaper for such
groups as pensioners or the unemployed.

Television for special payment, whether by coin or cable,
similarly would not help integration. It would increase social
inequality in an aspect of life where it has not been prominent thus
far. It would be hard to imagine the National Gallery charging a fee
of 10p for letting someone view the work of some minor painter but
charging £1 for a look at a painting by Botticelli. Markets do not
automatically provide diversity, multiplicity, inclusiveness or a
sense of social justice. They have their place but they need to be
supplemented by other mechanisms, and a pluralistic national and
regional broadcasting system financed in varying proportion by
fees, public revenues and advertising income might be one of them.

Another task is that of promotion of trust in the future. Without it
much of work, saving and having children become meaningless.
Another aspect of this problem is trust in the political community,
balancing honest reports about its shortcomings with equally
truthful reports about, as Mrs Williams put it, 'what politicians do
to deserve to be trusted'.

Truthfulness can be promoted on radio and television by showing
events in their true proportions against the statistical data of their
larger background, before giving a close-up of the particular
current change which necessarily generates an exaggerated impres-

sion if it is reported without this use of 'memory' for background information.

A broadcasting system should not pretend that conflicts do not exist but it could try to present rational ways for dealing with them. People must resist adversaries but they could take care to under-retaliate so as to avoid escalation. The cost-benefit balance of conflict could be shown: how cheap is Arab oil per barrel, if the expectable military costs for its continued security are added to the price? Will it still be cheaper than developing oil in other regions of the world or getting more energy from coal and other sources?

Broadcasting could help to make complex social systems and social problems more transparent, particularly with the help of television. It could offer a museum of possible futures for people to widen their horizons and equip themselves for possible choices.

A broadcasting system, in short, can make people more aware of themselves, of one another and of what they have in common. It can help them to become more aware of their community, of humankind, and of that reality which is greater than humankind. It can help us to make true a notion of the Greek philosopher Heraclitus: that each dreamer lives in a dream of his own but those who are awake have a real world in common.

8 Mary Douglas and Karen Wollaeger

Towards a Typology of the Viewing Public

Viewer's choices

Any good analysis of human behaviour should start with, end with, and never lose sight of the individual. It follows that this is also the right beginning for analysing viewers' choices. Too often the information available about individual viewers is too chaotic and mysterious to be of use to those concerned with broadcasting policy. Then some abstract entity such as the public or the prevailing cultural mood is invoked to fill the gap in theory, or a generalised creative energy, artistic style or bureaucratic authority is called in to represent the production side of the relation between the screen and the viewer. We will honour anthropological tradition which assumes that cultural trends can be traced to individual choices, which themselves result from pressures exerted by individuals upon one another.

This approach allows us to criticise a Nietzschean relic of nineteenth-century thinking which separates the artist's creative drive from authority. It is not helpful for us to give the creative artist a monopoly of that thing called style, and to separate his productive endeavour from his own deepest attitudes to authority, as if his inspiration was always bound to be at odds with social constraints. Each kind of authority has its aura, but there are many kinds; there is style in rejecting authority and style in accepting it, style in technology and style in every performance, whether in high culture or popular art, or in the everyday personal rituals of dressing and eating. Our method for identifying parts of the viewing public is to trace style changes that accompany changes in individual ideas about authority. We hope to place the usual questions about the public responsibilities of television in a new context, turning them back first to deeper problems in aesthetic theory.

For example, what should we think about the harm children may suffer by exposure to television violence? We have looked at representative research on that important topic and find that it treats violence, style and authority in separate compartments, without justifying the underlying assumptions. Everyone knows that some violence on the screen is not alarming, while some off-screen hints of violence are terrifying. What may harm children is the message about authority as much as the sight of violence as such. We need a better typology of the viewing public and its experience of authority.

Difficulties of television research in the United States

Television audience research has been problematical from the beginning. One of the biggest problems with research to date is that there has been no consistent typology of programmes. While it is assumed that programmes can be grouped in such a way that content and cast members can be seen to be attracting similar audiences, there has been no consistent means developed for characterising the content and its relation to audience segments.

Studies which derive typologies statistically[1] have so far failed to provide criteria that would enable new programmes to be placed within their typologies. Lacking a theory of types, there is no guarantee that a typology relates to anything except the imagination of the typologist. Programme types tend to be narrowly defined by a small number of programmes so that when these particular programmes go off the air the type no longer exists. The typology in general does little more than reiterate labels applied to shows by programmers and TV listings. Lacking theoretical underpinning, the typology is useless when programming changes, providing no guidelines for placing a programme in one category or another. These problems are typical of attempts to relate viewer characteristics to types of programming.

We are proposing a new anthropological approach to identifying audience segments. We assume that television series are part of a social process in which there is some interaction between audience, distributors and producers. We assume that in the long run this interaction should result in a flexible adaptation of styles and plots to audience segments. This mutual adaptation is seen through various kinds of rating systems, and results in the creation of public mythologies that express, to varying degrees, values and norms shared by large numbers of people.

In a sense we are doing research on life-styles. This is without apologies to the people in market research who have been trying to identify life-styles for commercial purposes and for television analysis. Though they do identify life-styles satisfactorily, they fail to locate them or explain them. The main problem with audience research in the United States is that the information provided by psychographic or life-style measures is vast and difficult to interpret without a theoretical framework. Consequently, a potentially rich source of information on the relationship between viewer characteristics and programming is virtually ignored. Though audience research is generally constructed on principles that are meant to cut across the usual divisions by social class, education and income, no typology so far produced can account for the comedian whose jokes reach right through the class structure. This paper indicates how to find vertical sections in which are associated people who share basic interests in common, cutting right down through the layers of social stratification.

Vertical cuts in the viewing population

Since existing market research and all social survey is designed to slot behaviour and attitudes into the horizontal scheme of class stratification, there is no way of finding our vertical sectors of the public in it. Yet, if we really want to understand style, we have to look for them because we argue that divisions based upon attitudes for and against the central authority, wherever that may be located, are the strongest clues to stylistic differences. Surely we should not deny the importance of the unequal horizontal stratification which is maintained by industrial society. We do not deny the vital significance of class inequalities. We try constantly to be aware of the tremendous pressures and constraints imposed by industrial society and its stratified social system. However, sociology today needs a much finer analysis of the relation between infrastructure and superstructure. By sorting out attitudes to authority we may be able to reach an understanding of stylistic differences which is obscured by any analysis of social class conducted by the upper stratum. We undertake to show that all the way down the class structure we can make vertical cuts that would reveal a stable typology of viewers. One would be a like-minded tradition-bound officialdom, from top bureaucracy down to the Post Office counter. Another vertical cut would reveal wild cards among some less-esteemed professions, such as the construction workers, who used to form the lump of individualists who rejected unions and national insurance. Their life-style would be distinctive, ocean-fishing, hearty drinking, expensive cars and clothes, all the while relishing their chosen insecurity. Among this section we can also recognise Jeremy Isaacs' inventive producers and reporters fretting at authority's bumbling constraints. These two cuts correspond closely to a scheme already found useful for analysing culture. It is a two-dimensional scheme which gives four extreme types of roles, each type interlocked with a pattern of moral judgements that sustain the roles.

FIGURE 1: *A grid group approach to TV programming*
In order to relate a typology of TV dramas to one of public taste, it will be helpful to define social contexts. Here we apply the classification of contexts based on grid/group analysis which defines a field of social constraints. The diagram illustrates four different kinds of social context. Along the vertical dimension a form of constraints we call grid controls the individual through the construction of progressively more precisely defined social categories. Along the horizontal dimension, social constaints are engendered by affiliation with a social body. The interaction of these two dimensions defines four social contexts in which different patterns of rewards and penalties and their moral justifications arise.

B		C
Insulated individuals	Hierarchical groups	
Enterprising individuals	Egalitarian groups	
A	D	

Social context A, low grid, low group—Individualist competitive, entrepreneurial.
Social context B, high grid, low group—Individualist controlled by classifications from A.
Social context C, high grid, high group—Collectivist, hierarchical organisation with strong internal loyalties.
Social context D, low grid, high group—Collectivist, small group, egalitarian, covert internal competition.

This diagram represents an argument developed in M. Douglas, *Cultural Bias* (Royal Anthropological Institute London, 1978).

For the first cut let us start with those who are entirely on the receiving end of authority, whose main experience is of constraints by rules that other people make. These insulated individuals who are most thoroughly constrained are at the top left-hand corner of Figure 1. In modern industrial society this might be the vast majority, which according to the usual sociological view constitutes the bottom layer of a horizontal class structure. But we can suggest many places where there are people who feel that their lives are constrained by rules that other people make, and who, according to class criteria, might seem to be located fairly high up the horizontal system of classification.

The second vertical cut shows, on the bottom right-hand corner of Figure 1, the small groups of dissenters, often intellectual cliques or religious sects, withdrawn from the great mainstream dialogue about how authority should be exerted. At the top left-hand corner, the insulated individual is withdrawn from the dialogue just because he/she is insulated; the dissenters on the bottom right have taken some initiative to take away from the diagram that diagonal from B to D. We are left with two more types, on the top right, hierarchised, compartmentalised officialdom; on the bottom left the individualists, creative in various special ways, reaching out to wide constituencies and finding authority particularly obtuse and obstructive. Since we know who these people are and can recognise them, should we not ask what they like to see on the screen and hear on the radio? What are their viewing tastes? Assume that their roles in work, sooner or later, by choice or by training, are matched to their personalities, presumably when they switch on they find some shows more congenial, more close to their own reality, expressing their own concerns and sensibilities, and others more alien to their life-styles. We will seek to identify viewing preferences that might be related to the life-styles which encapsulate these particular experiences of authority.

Anthropological models

We found the stimulus for this work from two important studies from social anthropology dealing with forms of popular entertainment; first, James Peacock's study of the Indonesian proletarian drama as a rite of modernisation[2] and second, Don Handelman's analysis of public events as they reflect on the social environment.[3]

Peacock shows that Southeast Asia supports at least twenty times the number of professional drama troupes per capita that we do in the United States and that theatre in Southeast Asia continues to exist as a crucial mass medium. The Javanese he studied paid for entertainment that expressed certain facets of their lives: a concern for national progress and harmony; the pains of progress and of present conditions; and desires for romantic freedom and personal success. Plots expressing these concerns could be divided into two types that showed consistent regularities in outcome, agencies of outcome, setting and time spans. He distinguished these plots as being traditional T-plots, concerned with commenting on the *status quo*, and modernising M-plots, concerned with linear, goal-oriented behaviour. While the T-plot follows individuals through traditional life stages, elaborating on appropriate relationships, and pointing out along the way what is inappropriate, the M-plot follows an individual from the traditional proletarian environment into the world of the urban élite. One is concerned with reconciling the way things are, while the other tells a story of fortuitous escape. The modernisation of Java was reflected in Peacock's study by the rapid spread of new M-plots from one troupe to another, while new T-plots failed to be adopted.

The dominant theme of both plot types at the time of Peacock's study was achieving élite-proletarian marriage. In T-plots blood bonds override individual preferences, restricting the scope of the individual for negotiating his own future. Élite-proletarian marriages are broken up by élite parents and husband and wife, parent and child are separated in a heart-rending scene. Reconciliation is achieved only in the next generation when the proletariat-élite child is accepted into the élite household. No new household is formed in the T-plot. Settings are traditional. Evil, embodied in the élite parent, is accepted, rather than punished, as élite superiority is part of the social structure.

In M-plots, proletarian blood bonds are broken, leaving the individual free to 'marry up' and form a new household. The opportunity presents itself through sheer luck and is furthered by the sexual attractiveness of the proletarian. To secure his new place in the world, the proletarian must sever relations with his old class. Accordingly, some former friend or relative is portrayed throughout the play as increasingly evil until the audience is able to cheer wholeheartedly at the end when he is seen receiving his punishment as the proletariat-élite couple are joined. In M-plots events take place in modern urban environments and characters are urban and modern in dress and manner. Marriage is achieved in a matter of weeks or months, and the story does not concern itself with the next generation. M-plots are more likely to use killings as a means of moving the story along, and less likely to exploit the pathos of victims. In general, movement in M-plots is likely to be individual and innovative, while movement in T-plots is institutional and cyclical.

TABLE 1 Peacock's comparison of T- and M-plots in melodramatic stories

	Type-T	*Type-M*
Status of main characters	Proletariat and élite	Proletariat and élite
Initial goals of main characters	Proletariat-élite marriage	Proletariat-élite marriage
Outcome of story	Proletariat-élite marriage negated, élite blood bonds affirmed	Proletariat-élite marriage affirmed, proletariat blood bonds negated
Agency which brings about story's outcome	Blood bond between élite and half-élite plus fate, which opposes personal choices	Personal responses (partly sexual) or proletariat and élite characters plus luck which furnishes opportunities
Setting	Traditional Java	Modern urban Indonesia
Time to bring about outcome	15–30 years	Weeks or months

The audience for the Javanese proletarian drama is much simpler to grasp than TV audiences. Peacock characterises the Ludruk audience as mostly older proletarians whose social mobility is extremely low. The Ludruk M-plot encourages its audience to participate vicariously in the modernisation process, encouraging it to think in a linear rather than a cyclical fashion. The formula is that of late eighteenth-century romantic novels like *Tom Jones* or *Moll Flanders*. The kind of action encouraged by such stories is linear, continuous and goal-oriented. Although the Ludruk audience is doomed to frustration by its own lack of mobility, it is fascinated by a kind of goal-oriented action which, according to Peacock, is well adapted for enabling it to propel its children into the modern world.

While Peacock's model provides an excellent preliminary framework for examining some stylistic aspects of TV drama, the diversity of dramatic series types and audiences for TV demands a more complex formulation.

Now we turn to Don Handelman, who has proposed a model of levels of reflexivity in cultural events which is useful here. Handelman's model relates dramatic form and the self-awareness that can be reflected in cultural events to the social environment in which they occur. Handelman's first distinction rests on levels of audience involvement. The audience is active or passive to the degree that the entertainment reflects upon the categories that organise its experience. A cultural event may comment in very complex ways on the daily lives of participants, it may simply reiterate well-known categories, or it may comment on worlds that bear very little relation to participants' lives. In any case participants will carry information from cultural events into their lives.

Handelman suggests that different cultural events encourage the freeing of the self in varying degrees and with different foci, and that these variations in focus are related to social context. Handelman states that:

> Through play, the self is freed from the ideal and real strictures of cosmic and social order. In this state, the self becomes open to receive those messages which are commentaries on its situation in everyday life. Within play, the self as subject can regard itself and others as object. This loss of, or distancing from, subjectivity permits one to gain unusual perspectives on oneself, on oneself in relation to others, and on oneself in relation to the principles of order.

While the phenomenon of television itself may relate most clearly to Handelman's category of spectacle, in which the individual participates largely through identification with the protagonist, messages embedded in TV series contain elements similar to Handelman's other cultural events: festival, dyadic joking and rites of reversal. As Handelman states it, the reflexive self is most active in festival events involving rites of reversal which reflect in a complex manner on highly organised categories within a group. The festival may reflect on the overall unity of a highly differentiated group by dissolving and restoring internal lines and symbolically acting out the contradictions inherent in a highly structured social environment. In less highly structured group environments, where clear internal divisions are minimal, there is less scope for reflection on internal categories, and ritual play is more likely to consist of reaffirmation of external boundaries and the exorcism of bad feelings within the group. Handelman predicts that in social contexts less dependent on group affiliation, there will be less active reflection on social categories. In these contexts entertainment tends either simply to repeat familiar categories, or to move into a realm of fantasy.

Compared with Peacock's Ludruk T-plots, the lower level of reflexivity in the Ludruk M-plots corresponds to Handelman's predictions about social context. In a modernising society with its increasing specialisation and dissolution of group boundaries he would expect a lower level of reflexivity in entertainment. We would explain this by saying that where social boundaries are dissolving or in transition, it is stories of action and individual goals rather than of social groups and structure that tend to be generated.

A typology of television dramas

Assuming an interaction between audience, producers and product, it is possible to recognise some aspects of the popular mythology which would emerge from each social context outlined above, and to hazard some predictions about how a particular type of drama might contain elements that would appeal to viewers subject to specific social constraints.

We divide television dramas into two main categories according to whether they bring to the foreground the structure of social relations, or bring forward action and short-term goals. Attitudes to modernisation, either hopeful and approving, or pessimistic, give further subdivisions. The typology can be summarised as follows:

A. *Concerned with the structure of social relations*
One type of drama in this class focuses on social harmony. Its characteristics are concentration on clear internal role patterns; the group is valued positively; there is an optimistic attitude to change; the same characters reappear through series; style attempts realistic portrayal, e.g. *Upstairs, Downstairs, Lou Grant, The Duchess of Duke Street, Dallas.* The second type of drama in this class portrays disruption and intrusion. It is characterised by concentration on the ambiguities of internal role structure, social disruptions and supernatural intrustions. Portrayals are stylised allegories, e.g. *Mary Hartman, Mary Hartman, The Prisoner.*

B. *Concerned with goals and action*
One type of drama in this class reflects endlessly on routine and on magical escapes from routine. The focus is on rules and rule transgression, characters concerned with working towards highly role-specific goals (e.g. police) or with fantasy escapes from everyday roles; the same team interacts with new cast in each episode, e.g. *Quincy, Charlie's Angels, Kojak.* The second type in this class is individual quest: the spontaneous creation of new roles and situations; goals which have to do with freedom and personal success; the same individual (or pair) with new cast in each episode, often opposing themselves to powerful multinational organisations, e.g. *Starsky and Hutch, The Avengers.*

Concerned with the Structure of Social Relations

Our first set of TV dramas places social interactions in the foreground and individual, goal-oriented actions in the background, providing the means by which structure or problems in social relations are lighted up. Here the audience is actively involved in piecing out relationships between people and between events rather than following an individual or team through a series of actions. One of two categories of drama in this set we call dramas of social harmony, because the aim seems to be to reconcile hostile or antithetical elements in social life. By contrast, another category can be distinguished which we call dramas of disruption and intrusion. The aim of the latter is more often to point at danger from irreconcilable elements.

Dramas of social harmony

In the drama of social harmony the reconciliation of seemingly anomalous elements in the society is achieved by defusing perceived dangers. This is accomplished by pointing out the ridiculousness of extreme positions through either humorous juxtapositions and reversals, or logical exposition. These dramas reflect a social environment perceived as highly structured, where exchanges between social groups are valued positively and well-regulated rules about exchange and the rules of social structure are mutually reinforcing. This corresponds to the experiences likely to arise in our social context C in Figure 1. Because the individual in this context feels certain of the ordering of his social world, he is freer than individuals in other contexts to question and reflect on this order without defining himself as marginal. Dramas of social harmony may reflect on extremist positions or contradictions within the accepted order without seriously questioning the ultimate goodness of that order. The early episodes of *All in the Family* and its English predecessor, *Till Death do us Part*, are an excellent example of humorous reflections of this sort, presenting families of extreme stereotypes: male and female, youth and middle age, and confronting them with other stereotypes, often turning the tables on their expectations, but ultimately poking fun at the weaknesses of each extreme.

Dramas of social harmony are, like Peacock's T-plots, more concerned with commenting on existing structure than with ends and means. Many mysteries which piece together a coherent view of seemingly disparate groups should be placed in this category. The screening process of this cosmology with its bias against admitting irreconcilable evils, may sometimes tend to minimise evil.

We observe that in dramas of social harmony perceptions of nature are constructed with hierarchical categories which reflect the *status quo*. Social groups are depicted as having regulated crossing points where appropriate exchanges take place. Accordingly, nature and culture are not contrasted; rather, one is seen as reflecting the other through metaphors of structural match in which nature is clearly organised on the same principles as the social structure. Films like *Lassie* or *Black Beauty*, where a special breed of animal bears the stamp of aristocracy, are typical of a style of presenting nature in which its real glories are always highly cultured.

The camera returns to particular personal and cultural landmarks which reappear throughout the series and which accumulate historical and personal significance within the story. Space is also organised as a metaphor for social relations. The structure of space in social harmony programmes like *Upstairs, Downstairs* presents an unproblematic structural fit between the spatial and the social order. Action takes place in a limited number of locations which recur. Behaviour is appropriately varied for place and sense of place tends to be static so that there are few scenes of transit. When characters are in transit, space tends to retain its structure and static quality, as on cruise ships.

This is the only one of the four types which attempts to present a coherent picture of space abroad. Space abroad is understandable in terms of the structure of space at home. When characters travel abroad, most of the humour comes out of their efforts to make sense of the rules there. Contact with abroad is seen as instructive and beneficial, a source of material and cultural enrichment.

The time span of action in dramas of social harmony is long, spanning years. Series tend to include at least three generations, signifying the ongoing nature of the community. Passage of time is represented by births, deaths, marriages and social changes. Rather than signifying the co-existence of past and present through flashback techniques, the past is represented through the ageing of characters, by familiar landmarks which draw attention to past events in the story. Continuity between past, present and future is emphasised. Time is represented as an orderly continuum and the camera moves from scene to scene according to orderly, temporally coherent rules. There is no rapid shifting between scenes. Episodes are built upon past episodes so that the context of the viewer in terms of remembered time becomes synonymous with that of the protagonists as in *Upstairs, Downstairs*. That the representation of time is almost wholly social is evident in the even lighting of the scenes, which plays down the minor calendrical changes of night and day.

Where violence enters into this category of programmes it is used to bring about restitution and remedies, and violence itself seldom occurs on screen. An ultimate faith in mediating institutions is expressed in these series and bad guys are seen as fallen but socially redeemable. Sex in these dramas tends to be seen as an element that is both personal and social. When it is important to the story, emphasis will be on efforts to keep these aspects in balance. Dramatic series in this category tend to be family sagas including several generations, like *Dallas* or *The Archers*. They tend to focus on rites of passage like births, deaths, graduations and marriages.

Dramas of disruption

Unlike the dramas of social harmony, dramas of disruption and intrusion explore pessimistic attitudes towards nature and society. They deal with dangerous intrusive elements that cannot be reconciled. These intrusive elements may be represented by disrupted personal relations within a group caused by ambiguities in its internal role structure, or by intrusive outside elements. In these stories things are never what they appear or ought to be. Expected relationships are often reversed. Husbands and wives or parents and children may become bitter enemies because of intrinsically evil natures or possession by outside forces. Focus is usually on a loosely organised group of people and danger to the group or individuals within it from some evil force.

When the boundary between insiders and outsiders must be constantly reinforced, then the style emphasises strong contrasts between good and dangerous elements in culture and nature. Instead of complex metaphors, we are given repeatedly under-scored contrasts between natural and unnatural events. In these dramas both nature and human beings are capable of harbouring dangerous intrusive elements.

A stylistic feature for this type is the way the camera loads space with meanings. Well-known historical landmarks are ignored in favour of mysterious, little-known ones, so that space takes its meaning from the context of the story. Contrasts between safe and dangerous or interior and exterior space are emphasised. Bright and dark contrast reinforce the emphasis. The camera may repeatedly shift perspective on a scene reinforcing the effect of circular space; lenses emphasise depth of field rather than panoramic expanses.

Abroad is represented as dangerous and mysterious. Its danger is represented either by focusing on an intrusion into the centre space from abroad (by a human being, mysterious supernatural or technological elements, or elements from outer space) or by an intrusion into dangerously affective space by protagonists (wild nature, outer space, ancient or primitive places). To take an illustration from *The China Syndrome*, the central space is suddenly capable of massive contamination and yet remains the only place where safety can be achieved; death and pursuit lurk on the outside and the audience views the final crisis from the margin of a centre which is finally invaded and decontaminated. Even the title suggests a concern with bursting boundaries; the China Syndrome means a catastrophe that would burn through the earth's core to China.

In dramas of disruption and intrusion place is also bound up with identity. Intrusions by foreign elements or intrusion into alien places are likely to result in undesirable transformations; the creation of the pathetic monsters of post-war Japanese horror films, or the loss of identity by amnesia when a character crosses the boundary of the familiar. Intrusion may also result in some moral-technological cataclysm resulting in the destruction or dehuman-isation of the human race.

Sex in these series is seen as a possibly anti-social force which might emerge at any time to disrupt social relations. Ambition is treated in much the same way. The themes present a constant war between the personal and the social. Characters are presented as allegorical figures representing particular virtues and vices.

The disruption and intrusion stories with supernatural elements, rather than blaming human nature for troubles, blame intrusive supernatural forces. The supernatural story is linear, building fear and horror of intrusion to the highest pitch possible by adding elements of disorder until it is resolved by destruction of the evil. Here the evil is never really destroyed, but subdued in its current manifestation. Good does not triumph, but is reminded of the necessity and near futility of constant vigilance. Nor is order completely restored. As in the first subset, something very valuable has been lost, innocence and an innate belief in goodness and ultimate order in the universe.

The time span of action in dramas of disruption and intrusion tends to be shorter than in dramas of social harmony, usually encompassing only days or weeks. The programme seems to assume that characters inhabit time resembling that which the audience inhabits, but that crises follow one another more quickly. A single episode is likely to focus on one or two days and a string of episodes making up a vignette usually extends for a few weeks at the most.

There may be flashes forward and backward in time as well as shifts between simultaneously occurring scenes. Perceptions of time in these series are personal. The audience may be allowed into a protagonist's mind where it hears echoes of past or future events. These series do not present time as a continuum as in the dramas of social harmony, where there is a clear historical dimension. Any reference to history is to very ancient and occult history exerting power in the present of the story. The story itself may be located in any historical or future period.

Because its subject is the physical manifestation of the unseen, the supernatural story may show a great deal of overt physical violence. The manifestation of violence often begins with physical anomaly (telekinesis, unidentifiable or misplaced sounds and objects) escalating into horrible impacts which may be full of blood and gore towards the end. In keeping with the theme of deceptive innocence, the evil often attacks through children or women. In these supernatural stories fears about the uncontrollable and corrupting nature of sex or power are likely to be expressed through dangerous children. In television series of this type most of the cast changes from episode to episode. Perhaps the supernatural experiences are so extraordinary that it might be straining the bounds of a credible story to keep the same supporting cast. Episodes are framed by a narrator or linked to a single figure, maintaining continuity and assuring us that what we are about to see is fantastic but true.

Concerned with Goals and Action

This second class of television dramas is expected to correspond to the left-hand side of Figure 1, where group membership is weak and individuals are either insulated from others by social classifications, or expected to stand on their own feet in a competitive world. These dramas place action in the foreground and the structure of social relations in the background. Accordingly the focus is narrower, limited to a more specialised view of individuals or teams and paying less attention to their integration. Action is likely to arise from individual conflict and usually results in the domination of one by another. Here again we find two subsets: one reflection on routine (and escapes from routine) and the other following individual quests.

Routine-reconciled dramas

The routine-reconciled dramas unquestioningly identify right with accepted rules. The fantasy variant reverses the content of accepted categories (e.g. police become the bad guys, file clerk becomes boss), but both present a rule-oriented cognitive scheme.

In the routine-reconciled dramas characters are presented in fully defined, familiar roles which are manifestations of an institutional structure which may encompass or provide background to the action. Personal interaction between individuals performing different roles is at a very low level. Action in the drama consists of conflict between these formally defined role categories.

These dramas may be stories about individual rites of passage through rigorously defined stages in which deviation from the rule results in catastrophe. The protagonist has a single-minded goal which conflicts with other aspects of his life, forcing him to make a choice. Violence in this type of story tends to be ritual, portrayed in a controlled fashion as a necessary ordeal. Emphasis is on the value of endurance rather than the harmful effects of violence. Many sports success stories are of this type, especially boxing stories. They often include themes having to do with prison. These stories frequently appear on American television as mini-series with only three or four episodes. While they may have an obvious explanatory power for people whose lives are highly constrained by role categories, they may also have appeal for those who have managed to make their way out of such a situation.

Long-running series that emphasise rule reinforcement are often nominally about routine police work, like the old US *Dragnet* series and *Z-cars* in the UK. *Kojak* surely belongs here and no wonder he is a favourite in Buckingham Palace. Focus in these series is usually on a team that is galvanised into action only when a crime is reported. Crimes are discovered and solved through routine police work, rather than by any special craft. Violence is allowed to occur on screen and its presentation involves direct physical impacts—car crashes, fist fights, wrestling—ending in capture or death for the bad guys. While these programmes usually begin with the team on a routine patrol, rupture in routine and the actions which restore it are the real subject.

In the fantasy escapes from routine, social categories are held constant, but their valencies are reversed, often magically. In contrast to the supernatural dramas of disruption and intrusion, magical powers, when they occur here, are specific and controllable, harnessed for particular purposes. These powers are activated only in special situations, and there is no implication that they have any lasting influence on the disposition towards good or evil in the world.

Some of the fantasy escapes feature superpeople, capable of transcending their own physical boundaries for the sake of maintaining order. These dramas express discomfort with social constraints; they endow the usually powerless individual with superhuman strength which makes him more powerful than the institutions and technologies which dwarf him (mild-mannered Clark Kent becomes Superman, faster than a speeding bullet, able to leap tall buildings in a single bound). Violence that occurs on screen is often expressed in images of breaking through barriers or of threatening explosions and natural disasters shored up by the superheroes. This is effective violence, designed to produce excitement rather than fear. The viewer knows that the superperson always prevails. The superperson is so strong that hand-to-hand combat is pointless. He/she prevents catastrophe and rounds up the criminals. The superperson is also so strong that sex is impossible. His/her sexuality may be ignored or played up by physical attributes that are exaggerated when superpower is activated, so that sexuality is emblematic and part of an impersonal force for good rather than an aspect of personal relations with others. The more the superhero is unexpectedly involved with very powerful enemies and international affairs, the more the story may appeal to an audience of enterprising individuals. Other programmes state clearly that they are dealing with fantasy escapes, presenting magical places where dreams that reverse one's real prospects in life can be lived out. In these, justice is meted out in a magical landscape where all goes well for the deserving, and the undeserving get their true deserts. Rod Serling sometimes produced stories of this type for *The Twilight Zone* as well as dramas of disruption and intrusion.

All routine/fantasy escape dramas show a strong unquestioning moral bias in dealing with punishment and justice. Their themes treat of containment of disorderly forces or escape from unfair restrictions.

Already we have said enough to indicate how closely meshed is the style with the plot and characterisation and how all flow from basic attitudes to authority. When a vulnerable majority is seen to be threatened by an unprincipled few, regulation is by coercion. Then stylistic contrasts are framed in idioms of vulnerability and strength, a common motif in our routine/magical escape type of dramas. Nature is allied with images of gentle, vulnerable things: women, children and helpless animals, all in need of protection. Weakness and vulnerability are opposed to strength and toughness. In women, children, animals, and the sick or crippled, weakness and vulnerability are expected. In men in their prime such traits are unforgivable. So the stool pigeon gets the worst of it again and again.

Just as personality is weakly developed, so do we find that space is impersonal. The camera in routine/magical escape dramas takes the viewpoint of a third person accompanying protagonists closely (in the old *Dragnet* series the viewer is initially placed in the back seat of the police car). There is little shifting back and forth between various scenes; rather, the viewer follows protagonists through what seems to be real space. Settings are usually modern urban, and realistic. Focus is usually on institutional or public life, rather than home life, and these domains are kept separate. The protagonists' activities are prescribed by role-related rules relating time, place and function. The old *Dragnet* series is a good example of this, beginning and ending with a report of time and location, order disrupted and restored. Protagonists here never stray from their beat.

In the magical escape varieties the individual temporarily transcends the routine of daily life by entering a magical place where many of the realities of home are reversed. Space in the magical setting metaphorically reiterates the structure of space at home. However, use of the camera becomes more like that in dramas of social harmony as magical space is invested with more significance than ordinary space. In *The Wizard of Oz* we are given both the routine and the escape. Dorothy runs away from the boring routine and petty injustices of farm life where no-one seems to have time for her, and finds herself in a magical Kansas where scarecrows and trees talk, and where witches ride broomsticks. The space in her escape is structured like the space she left, but invested with magical properties. TV's *Fantasy Island* and *The Love Boat* present a similar magical-moral place where people are chastened about their attitudes to the world they inhabit daily. Abroad in this context is spectacularly exotic, but its spatial structure simply reiterates reality.

The time-span of the action in these dramas of routine/magical escape is short, covering hours or days. This is the result of an emphasis on short-term, usually role-defined goals. There is little shifting between simultaneously occurring scenes except at specific moments when beating the clock becomes important, as when Superman or Wonder Woman is about to save someone. Shifting back and forth in time never occurs in these dramas, although in the dramas of magical escape the protagonist may be temporarily transported outside of time by magic or a dream state. The absence of shifting in time is related to the impersonal stance taken by the camera (perhaps because this implies subjective experience, while time in these dramas is one of the objective rule-setting elements).

In these routine/magical escape dramas violence occurs on screen, but although it seems to entail direct impacts, there is usually little blood, disorder or inarticulate human sounds of pain. Violence is committed by both good and bad guys, and good as well as bad may be killed. The death of a criminal (bad guys are, of course, criminals) may be mildly affective, demonstrating the wages of sin, as in *Bonanza* or *The Untouchables*, when a misfit leaves the good guys no choice but to kill him. Violence here tends to be an effective means of maintaining order.

Dramas of individual quest

Here we find a world of individuals engaged in competitive strategies in order to achieve goals related to personal freedom or success. Spontaneity and innovation are highly valued in these dramas. At their extreme, dramas of individual quest tend to take place in a borderless international scene where local variations exist only to provide a colourful backdrop for the action. Some police and detective series also fit into this category. Protagonists show much more autonomy than in the routine-reconciled dramas, relying on friends and contacts from all walks of life to help solve crimes. The law often tends to be subordinated to personal ethics. The ideal in these dramas is extreme rationality and detachment. Facial expressions are kept to a minimum, and death is nothing more than a calculated risk.

Sex in these dramas is often dangerous; no one is completely trustworthy in this environment because of conflicting loyalties. Relationships are often cancelled by death and sudden disappearance. Those dying or disappearing are often women, because this is usually presented as a man's world where very powerful women figure only among the bad guys. In Peacock's terms these are pure M-plots; human relations are entirely contractual, settings modern, strategy all-important and time-spans short. Individuals often seem to be operating in limitless space, and not only bloodbonds but personal relations of any kind are often negated as soon as formed. *Kung Fu* is the extreme of this kind of drama. These dramas reflect the context of individualist enterprise. Handelman says of this kind of entertainment:

> Particularly in this context, media of mass entertainment encourage the perpetuation of the dyadic relationship between the spectator and the performer. Thus large numbers of people remain quite individuated, even when together, while they passively absorb dramatic projections which themselves do not necessarily reflect on any reality known to these spectators.

The enemy in these programmes often turns out to be a multinational corporation. The leader of the corporation may appear to be foreign but often of no particular ethnic background. His cohorts are always of exotic origin, often oriental or middle-eastern, and are portrayed as cruel buffoons who are nearly powerless without instruction from their chief. In these dramas the protagonist is pitted against powerful coalitions while the organisation that he is presumably allied with remains in the background, seldom seen. This aspect of the drama of individual quest reflects an individualist cosmology. With dispersed and often tenuous alliances of common interest, the individual in this context is likely to elaborate on the perceived power and centralised authority of other groups. While the protagonist may hardly set foot in, or explicitly refer to, his own country throughout the action, his individual person, handsome, clean, elegant and resourceful, defines an invisible we that opposes itself to an unethical, vulgar and inhumane them, as in James Bond films and certain episodes of TV series such as *Charlie's Angels*.

Little as these series reflect on any reality known to them, the audience is offered incidental messages about contemporary life. Common prejudices about minorities or women or the availability and pervasiveness of particular standards of living are passed along in these series as established beliefs about the world we inhibit.

In this context each individual is consciously aiming to maximise his receipts. As there are few rules to observe, good and bad characteristics cannot be shown through respect for rules. Instead the clues which help the viewer to align villains and heroes are outward signs of vulgarity or refinement. In these dramas there are neither explicit boundaries defining social groups nor regulated crossing points for exchange to take place. Each unknown person must be sounded out individually as to trustworthiness, and outward clues can often be misleading. Humans are more likely to control than to be at the mercy of nature. However, there is an ethic of respect for nature which makes overexploitation or elaboration appear vulgar. This helps the contrast of vulgar and refined characters and settings, as in the contrast between the character of James Bond and that of Goldfinger. Vulgarity is often associated with separate ethnic or regional groups and refinement is the good, natural state of the unreflecting viewer's own country.

In dramas of individual quest space is not invested with deliberate personal or social meanings. The eye of the camera is impersonal, given to scanning the area of action before focusing it. Space appears rather flat, though close and far perspectives are contrasted.

Action takes place mostly abroad. Space abroad is controlled, often internationally, by various coalitions, not necessarily legal. Boundaries are crossed easily and spontaneously without passport, currency or language problems. While it is easy to go abroad and taken for granted that the protagonist spends most of his time there, being abroad is always risky. As in dramas of social harmony, the world abroad is seen as offering valuable benefits. They are more often material than cultural and must be taken by force or cunning. In these dramas, unlike those of social harmony, wherever home is the camera spends very little time there. Highways, waterways, railways, the sky and unlimited vistas make up a large part of the spatial imagery. Any place where the protagonist stops is likely to be a trap, and the only private space he enters (after he has been roused from his bed for a mission) is that of the enemy, often a garish technological fortress. While dramas of social harmony emphasise the foreign order and coherence of space abroad, dramas of individual quest stress bizarre and disorderly traits of alien territory. Information, goods and often women are at issue and the territory is charted out with a view to these. Early Fritz Lang films like *The Spider* are typical extremes of the drama of individual quest. In *The*

Spider an elegant young man finds a message with a map in a bottle while yachting at home. This sends him off to an exotic, barbaric remnant of Inca civilisation in South America, where he finds himself battling against an international conspiracy and returns home with a beautiful priestess rescued from her barbaric culture, who is then murdered by his enemies, setting him off on another quest, this time to an exotic, barbaric Middle East. Dramas of individual quest may also take place within one country, often involving a roaming individual or pair who become spontaneously involved in various situations which put them at odds with local law enforcement groups. Here abroad is reached as soon as one crosses county or state lines.

As in the dramas of routine/magical escape the time-span of action is short, spanning hours or days (usually not more than two). There is more shifting between simultaneously occurring scenes throughout the story, either because the premium placed on time is higher, as in *Mission Impossible*, or because the action is extremely episodic with multiple foci. Curiously, there is very little shifting back and forth in time, perhaps to allow the camera to take an impersonal stance, scrutinising actions and their tangible results without moral bias.

Violence occurring on screen is usually a central feature of the action in these dramas, but the violence is routine, entailing neither fear nor anger on the part of the protagonists. It is formal, balletic and highly strategic as in kung fu fighting, or in combats using advanced technology. It is effective, highly abstract and there is no blood or disorder, or signs of pain. Violence seems more metaphorical than real in programmes like *Chips*. One might regard it as a metaphor for getting things done and behind one. Refined gadgetry is matched against the heavy and vulgar technology of the enemy.

In sum, here we find violence presented as a normal, effective part of a rationalised, entrepreneurial world. The elimination even of sympathetic characters involves little pathos, because there simply isn't time to pause and mourn, nor is the characterisation sufficiently developed to draw strong sympathy.

Experimental avenues

It should be kept in mind that this typology, which is drawn in discrete sections, really represents a continuum. Furthermore, deeper analysis of stylistic bias among the four types would have to focus on a particular and limited historical period of television production. The present typology was conceived on the basis of 1979 programming. It could be more narrowly focused by concentrating only on programmes dealing with law and transgression, or other genre selections. Our biggest problem is to demonstrate that this typology of dramas corresponds to our parallel typology of social life. If it bears the kind of relation to the world of viewers that we assume, specially designed research would be needed to make the demonstration.

Suppose this whole exercise is based on a misconception about the relation between the viewers' tastes and the responsiveness of the producers to ratings. Suppose neither the buyers nor the producers take any notice of reports on the viewers' preferences. Then it could still be interesting because it might go some way to explaining why one network gets on a winning streak and then later begins to lose out. On the one hand the producers, acting in the dark, could be fortuitously striking a chord that matches the life-experience of one of our vertical segments. Then, since they do not know how they have deserved success, they do not know how to maintain it. They could veer off course and so lose their winning position, or the audience could change composition since the relative size of our four vertical segments could shrink or swell, thus affecting the popularity ratings. Not knowing what has caused the slippage, the losing production unit probably fires its director and looks for one with a different outlook.

Then it would be very instructive to look at the structure of organisation in the channels and networks, assuming that the producers think that what they themselves like is what the general public likes. Both CBS and ABC are convinced that they are reaching the great throbbing heart of the American public. However, after running neck and neck with ABC for the better part of the 1979–80 season, CBS pulled ahead and on 20 April finally won its first rating's season since 1976. But they have no clue as to what makes one of them more popular at one time than the other. Without aid of research we hazard the idea that the CBS at present is more mandarin-like and hierarchical in its organisation. People stay there a long time, accept constraints and are committed to the place and traditions. By contrast, the ABC seems more of an ideal place for creative knight-errant individualists, irreverent of tradition and impatient of authority. Predictably, the CBS seems to supply the public with more dramas of social harmony, while the ABC believes the American public really prefers questing buddies, individuals backing success and adventure. If these caricatures of the organisations stand up to closer examination, we can start to say something more about the mass production of mythologies, concentrating on the production side instead of the viewers.

There is no guarantee that the mass mythologies generated by the technologies of the future will please the public living in that future. We realise that the new satellite technologies are big business. But this does not say that the writing and production of the dramas is organised according to the big-business methods that apply to the electronics developments. There will probably be production of the old Metro–Goldwyn–Mayer type, achieving impossibly grandiose effects, and resulting from big-business organisation. There will also be a hot search for scriptwriters and producers, easily hired and easily fired, who need their friends for continuity in jobs, and whose reputation and careers depend on winning prizes awarded by select committees in the profession. To the extent that production may be dominated by small cliques of close friends we would expect dramas of the social disruption and intrusion type to dominate. But we do not expect the majority of the viewing public to appreciate them. Given free choice, they would probably prefer the series on social harmony produced by the old BBC. If legislation were to curb small businesses and generally drive people out of the category of self-employed, we would have a larger population working anonymously in bureaucracies, whether for the government or in big corporations. Surely then the dramas of individual quest as now presented would lose their appeal, since few could plausibly identify with questing buddies or lone adventurers. In such a shift of the occupational structure we would expect more interest in dramas reflecting on routine and magical escapes and more on social harmony. Only those few working in the media would identify with the problems analysed in dramas of disruption and intrusion and individual quest. Ever-fragmenting individualist small groups who might control production as the new technology gets under way are likely to provide an endless series of dramas of those kinds or curious combinations of the two. Their themes are more congenial to viewers who feel out on their own in an incalculable but competitive environment, than to viewers whose occupation gives them little scope for risk and responsibility and who find their richest interests in family life.

Our next project will be devoted to trying to track genre shifting within the typology, and especially shifts between different detective fiction stories and different science fiction stories, trying to relate these stylistic shifts to major economic and political changes affecting the broadcasting industry over the years since 1965. We should not conclude this introduction to anthropological perspectives on broadcasting without pointing out that if these arguments are accepted, the whole discussion of quality is radically altered. The indissoluble relation between style and authority means that no fetish can be erected; no abstract notion of quality, unanchored in the social intentions of artists, has validity. As well as audience research, the aesthetic theory will have to be worked out anew.

NOTES

1. For example, D. Gensch and B. G. Ranganathan, 'Utilization of TV Program Content for the Purpose of Promotional Segmentation', *Journal of Marketing Research* (1974); R. E. Frank, J. C. Becknell and J. D. Clokey, 'Television Program Types', *Journal of Market Research* (1971).
2. J. Peacock, *Rites of Modernization: Symbolic and Social Aspects of Indonesian Proletarian Drama* (University of Chicago Press, Chicago, 1968).
3. D. Handelman, *Reflexivity in Festival and other Cultural Events* (Routledge and Kegan Paul, London, 1979).

Janet Morgan

Summary of the Discussion

This account follows the three themes of the symposium: authority, style and choice, each considered in relation to broadcasting and its future. The themes were taken up one by one and in each discussion it came about that the participants explored three aspects: what is understood by this term—authority, style or choice—where broadcasting is concerned? what paradoxes are revealed? what assumptions lie beneath the way we talk about authority, style and choice in relation to broadcasting? These deliberations led members of the symposium to consider what principles they believed it essential for broadcasters to follow, by what criteria broadcasting authorities should seek to operate. From there, the discussion turned to the last question: what sort of broadcasting systems will be most likely to cherish such principles and follow such criteria? Indeed, what type of broadcasting systems will allow and encourage debate about exactly those issues which the symposium sought to understand: the meaning we give to 'authority', 'style' and 'choice'; the paradoxes we perceive; and the underlying assumptions we make.

In unravelling the question of authority in relation to broadcasting, members of the symposium drew out two strong threads. One, which I will turn to in a moment, concerned the nature of the institutions established by the government to control the operation of broadcasting media, to circumscribe their immense power, to shape their behaviour. The other dealt with the way in which the broadcasters themselves and the organisations in which they work use their opportunity to select, order and present programmes to a receptive audience. Though the two concepts are clearly interlocked—authority as it is exercised by the government towards the broadcasters and authority as it is exercised by the broadcasters towards the public—here they were pulled apart, examined and then brought together again.

Let us take the second question first: who are the broadcasters, the 'authorities' in the sense of 'authors'? Just as witnesses add weight to a story, so the broadcasters' imprint gives a report extra authority. Its impact is reinforced and not simply by what is put into the telling of a tale—details given, characters illuminated, circumstances illustrated, lessons drawn—but also by what is left out. All narrators are obliged to give shape and coherence to their stories; so too the broadcaster must select, trim, edit. He is, indeed, a 'presenter' of programmes. Even the most straightforward reporting of news is an exercise in establishing what is important and in what order and form it should be drawn to public attention. The audience can receive its programmes docilely, gratefully amazed. It can, on the other hand, be critical and thoughtful, seeking to appreciate the value of what it is getting and to understand why it is getting this in particular. A lively, intelligent public of the latter sort needs, therefore, to ask certain questions: for example, who are the producers of programmes and what is their particular stance? who, within the broadcasters' own professional hierarchy, is charged with the fundamental direction of the enterprise? what is the professional relationship between those whose chief business is to manage and those whose principal activity is to create? what sort of latitude or guidance is given to outsiders from whom work is commissioned? how are programmes influenced by the increasingly rule-bound circumstances in which they are prepared?

It has often been said (by Lord Reith, among others) that more of such wariness should be exercised by television viewers than by radio audiences. Television programmes do indeed have an extra ingredient—pictures—which adds to their authority to convince or bemuse. Television producers can certainly deploy a mysterious range of technical tricks, unlike those available to radio producers and possibly more various. Television may have greater power to trivialise or distort; audiences may find it harder to spot when this is happening. A suspicion that this is the case underlies much of the objection to that form of programme called 'faction' (or, as unhappily, 'docudrama'). Its detractors argue that broadcasters of such programmes are abusing the trust that is placed in them. Like a professional academic writer or a professional critic, a professional broadcaster must be explicit about the way in which he is putting his message across—is it a report of events that occurred? myth? analogy? metaphor? an account of imaginary happenings? If he neglects to make these explanations, if he muddles his audience, he risks undermining their confidence. He is abusing his authority and will, sooner or later, lose it. Worse; he is setting intellectual and ethical traps for himself. Professional reporters and critics try to be as honest as possible about their own motives—why am I transmitting this message? why do I judge in this way and not that way? what are my reasons for choosing this particular form of presentation? what does my audience need to know about me, my antecedents? am I bamboozling them? The broadcaster who confuses different types of narrative, who blurs the distinction between fiction and fact, is somehow *spongy*. The audience cannot be sure where they are with him and he may become unsure himself. Thus runs one set of arguments.

Those who support mixed forms (the usual term, 'genres', is hard on the ear and pretentious) answer both these points. In the first place, they observe, there are no pure ways of telling a story. Fiction and fact, drama and straight reporting, 'objective evidence' and 'subjective interpretation' are inextricably entwined. The broadcaster should certainly explain what he is aiming to do, and how, but he should not hesitate to try his audience with new devices. Only by doing so can he help to teach the public to recognise not just the factual elements in fiction but also the fictional elements in fact. As for the second point, the charge that employing mixed forms lays the broadcaster open to corruption, those who defend the practice argue that here the broadcaster is a true pioneer. All those who are professionally engaged in observing and describing behaviour— novelists, for example, or psychologists, anthropologists or historians—teach us that there are many ways of looking at the world and that perceptions and interpretations of particular phenomena, events, circumstances will vary enormously. The broadcaster, too, gives us new ways of perceiving and appraising. Mixed forms offer new insights.

That is the outline of the other set of arguments. Their proponents remind us that the most vociferous criticism of mixed forms has always been provoked by programmes dealing with subjects that are themselves contentious: the Suez episode, Islamic views of crime and punishment, the conduct and effects of certain government policies. 'Faction' is especially controversial when a programme challenges received thinking and accepted authority. Indeed, such moments are excellent opportunities for learning more about conflicts between two contenders for authority, two rivals who each claim to defend 'the public interest'—on the one hand, the government and, on the other, the broadcasters. This brings us back to the first of the symposium's two questions about authority: what is the relationship between the government and the media?

The discussion focused on Britain, partly because arrangements prevailing there were familiar to most of those who took part but also because of the special subtleties of the nature and operation of the system by which the government exerts its authority and the broadcasters assert their own. Why is it that in Britain the relationship is so vague, set out in language deliberately imprecise, sustained by discreet understanding and anticipated reaction, never explained exactly but constantly redefined, embodied in practice rather than theory? One suggestion is that, whereas countries with a written constitution are prone to adopt explicit regulations for the conduct of affairs and specifically to define the scope and limits of the State's authority, Britain's lack of a written constitution inclines her to proceed less precisely. Authority is not assigned but acquired, by custom and practice. Another view turns for a clue to the doctrine of the separation of powers. Where authority is divided, whether horizontally between federal, state or provincial and local governments, or vertically between executive, legislature and judiciary, each acting as a counterweight to the others, there we will find an explicit framework of regulations, provisions and procedures. In Britain the picture is blurred. Both these lines of argument are, perhaps, too elaborate. Maybe it is simply the case that, for reasons of history, geography, temperament, racial mixture, even climate, the British have on the whole preferred convention to regulation, muddling through to planning a route. The absence of detailed regulations delineating the relationship between the government and the broadcasters, stating in what circumstances, and how, the government might intervene in the production and transmission of programmes, does not follow from Britain's lack of a written constitution; both derive from a national tendency to pragmatism, a preference for seeking accommodation, a liking for smudged edges.

So how is it done? The keys are 'balance' and 'delegation'. Balance is attained thus. The government could make life impossible for the broadcasting authorities: it could deprive them of frequencies, starve them of money, require them to transmit, or not transmit, certain items or programmes. But self-interest, quite apart from any view of the public interest, deters politicians and officials from doing so. A Government may one day turn into an Opposition, and vice versa; politicians and officials may need protection from each other. All need public goodwill; they would never get away with open intervention, or not for long. Further, the government is uncomfortable with its authority, delegating it where it can. The governors of the BBC and the members of the IBA are not placemen; indeed, the government has occasionally embarrassed members of the two broadcasting organisations by inviting them to suggest nominees for these bodies, persons who can be relied upon to defend the interests of the broadcasting services. And the two organisations, soon to be augmented when the fourth channel comes into operation, are also expected to act as checks each upon the other and, at the same time, to offer each other mutual reinforcement. Even within the Cabinet, authority is largely delegated to the Home Secretary. It is considered unwise for the Prime Minister or Ministers collectively to be seen to be 'interfering' in this most sensitive of spheres.

How are these joints kept supple? Some participants in the symposium suggested that, where relations between the government and the broadcasting organisations are carefully regulated, there are also to be found complex and precise rules governing the provision of information. Like other privileges and duties, these rights and obligations are also spelt out. Again, this observation is illuminating but overcomplicated. Instead of following that trail, it is more helpful to look at a more basic phenomenon: trust, or the lack of it. Mutual trust is essential for the British system of delegated, balanced authority to work effectively. Broadcasters and government authorities must both be able to relax; each must be sure that there is a point beyond which the other will not go, beyond which the other will not exercise its power. For such assurance, something else is required: visibility. Each side must be reasonably certain of the motives, habits, doubts and fears and hopes of the other. That is why openness is important. Not a few critics maintain that there is, now, insufficient openness between the government and the broadcasters. Neither knows the cards the other has up his sleeve. Both become jumpy. Nerves are frayed.

To some extent both sides can substitute for openness with each other openness with a third party—the public. The government are publicly accountable; surely, the argument goes, the broadcasting authorities recognise that the public trust in the government's good sense will not be abused? The broadcasters look to the ratings; surely the government acknowledges that broadcasters would not jeopardise the trust of their audiences? But, of course, this is an exaggerated picture. In fact, we may inquire, how vulnerable are governments and how sensitive are broadcasters to public disapproval? Perhaps it is not so much the obvious moments of crisis in the relationship, after all, that we should be examining but everyday behaviour and ordinary attitudes. On what grounds, for example, does a government pretend to understand 'the public interest'? What supports the broadcasters' similar claim? Where do they, or might they, derive their particular legitimacy? These questions bring us to the second aspect of the discussion of authority: inherent paradoxes.

The first of these is obvious: those who enjoy real authority do not have to exercise it. It is more effective where it is not assertive but discreet. The moment at which the government openly confronts the broadcasters is one when quiet understandings have broken down. One side or the other knows that its authority has wavered; little wonder that it feels uneasy at being obliged to reclaim it. That is why—and here is the second paradox—arrangements for the allocation and exercise of authority are, in fact, devised to secure as much freedom as possible. The government and broadcasters are telling each other, as a parent or a schoolmaster might tell a child: 'Make up your own mind. I shan't stand in your way. But, if you make a mistake, the consequences will be dire.' But now it is necessary to remember another oddity: if arrangements for distributing, delegating and balancing authority are to be successful in practice, they must be both carefully designed and, at the same time, messy. Perfect hierarchies either become rigid or develop imperfections. Bureaucratic rituals either become stultifying or they are undermined by stratagems. The upshot of this is that both the government and the broadcasting authorities repeatedly find their stately procedures and considered responses eroded by confusion, hurry, error and chance.

It is as well that surprise constantly throws spanners in the works. Otherwise the legitimacy of existing arrangements would be less frequently questioned. There are, as the symposium was reminded, two important reasons why societies tend to accept authority as inevitable and proper. The first, a general truth, is that authority is a time-saver. Those over whom it is exercised are not obliged to test the content of every message, every instruction; instead, they can smartly proceed with the business of decision and action. Further, authority reassures. It promises that the choices it offers are legitimate and that they are compatible. 'Here is a bundle of opportunities', says authority; 'choose whichever you like. Don't worry; by selecting one you will not be sabotaging the rest. They all go together. As a matter of fact, they reinforce each other.' In this sense, 'authority' is like Edmund Burke's 'prejudice'. It saves effort and suppresses doubt. Here, indeed, are curious connections between authority and freedom.

What is the second reason why the legitimacy of institutional arrangements can so easily go unchallenged? It has to do with the complex and ambiguous nature of 'the public interest'. Take the particular case of the relationship between the government and the broadcaster. Each group regards itself as particularly well-equipped to discern where the public interest lies and to define what does, or does not, qualify as being part of it. Each group seeks public recognition for its own performance. 'The public interest' is established, public approval is sought, responses are fed back to the authorities, the definition is refined. But, as the symposium was forcefully told, this process is more closed, the atmosphere more claustrophobic, than we commonly care to admit. The very complexity of life—the fact that running a country and executing policy or running a broadcasting organisation and producing programmes—is *difficult* means that the task of describing and cherishing the public interest is, sometimes cheerfully, sometimes grudgingly, delegated to the authorities by that very public. 'The public interest' is not so much an elusive general good which the authorities set about recognising and protecting. It is more the product of competition between various counterbalancing forms of authority. Here is another paradox.

It brought the symposium to the third, and last, aspect of its effort to understand the concept of authority in the context of broadcasting: the attempt to recognise hidden assumptions. Discovering what is meant by the public interest led members of the conference to acknowledge that the authority claimed by government and broadcasters was not necessarily as legitimate as they would both wish to believe. Aristocratic ways of taking decisions — as to how people should conduct their lives or as to what sort of messages they should receive — have been succeeded by 'group monopolies'. Between those who utter and those who hear is a greater imbalance of authority than we popularly assume. We should think again about the nature and source of the broadcasters' claim to legitimacy.

It is also important to remember that these are questions about power. They concern political relationships. The technical complexities of the broadcasting process—from the operation of sophisticated electronic engineering to the manipulation of elaborate administrative rules—allow us to fall into the assumption that the problems broadcasters encounter are themselves technical and that the solutions lie in knowing how to manage money, machines, people. Governments adopt the same habits. We should, rather, prompt questions about power and influence—who is doing what to whom—and think less about administering existing arrangements and more about understanding attitudes.

If we fail to do so, we are assuming that our society already knows what it needs to know. That is a dangerous principle because it leads to ossification. To be creative, we should assume the opposite: that society does not yet know what it needs to know. We should recognise that we are engaged on a search, which is infinite. Since we must not waste time and energy, we need authority and coherence, the capacity to transfer knowledge and expertise already acquired and the capacity to co-ordinate action. But we have to marry authority and coherence with open-mindedness and opportunism; in seeking to understand how society tries to do this, the symposium was thus brought to the second theme of the conference: style.

Again, the starting point of the discussion was to try to discover what is understood by style, in relation to broadcasting. Not surprisingly, the linguistic aspects of style were explored first: the sort of language used by British radio and television broadcasters and the changes which it has undergone in the last fifty years. Until fairly recently the language and usage of radio and television programmes enjoyed, undoubtedly, greater linguistic authority than does the language of the press (with the possible exception of *The Times*, whose magisterial tone was, once upon a time at least, both the product and the property of the actual words and phrases its contributors used). Why was broadcasters' language and usage endowed with particular authority? How did this 'linguistic imperialism' come about? In part, of course, it derived from the fact that radio and television broadcasters addressed individual listeners and viewers directly, invading their homes. The public conversation was aimed towards private audiences. Then there was the all-pervasive, all-embracing nature of radio and television in general and the BBC service in particular: authors and performers were voraciously commissioned and their work, as much as that of the broadcasting services' own employees, followed the house style. Linguistic authority was, too, deliberately cultivated. Lord Reith consciously and vigorously believed in the therapeutic role of broadcasting. The purpose of programmes was to educate, as well as to inform and entertain.

These three characteristics are no longer so striking. It is to different groups in society that the broadcasting organisations seek to appeal, even to 'minorities' rather than to individuals. Instead of embossing all contributions with their own hallmark, the broadcasters try to adopt the style of the audiences they wish to attract, passing off as their own the language and habits of worlds 'outside'. As for high didactic purpose, that is something about which, sadly, the broadcasting authorities grew defensive and embarrassed. The symposium was to consider each of these developments in turn.

First, however, members looked more closely at the definition of style. It is, to a considerable extent, influenced by the technical opportunities and constraints of radio or television production. When new devices made it possible to insert filmed reports in news bulletins, that affected the manner of presenting the news. The speed at which images move influences the pace of spoken commentary, the numbers of words that can be delivered each minute. (And, similarly, grammatical structure can affect the way pictures are transmitted: German television, for example, tends to linger on an image while the audience awaits the verb at the end of a sentence.) The fact that radio and television programmes penetrate people's homes, where, moreover, they may be more generally accessible to children or where they may be chanced upon by the unsuspecting, presents broadcasters with special problems of propriety. Is foul language or the depiction of violence more offensive when it is transmitted by radio and television? Are such examples more forceful? When they came to consider institutional changes, members of the symposium were particularly anxious to find ways in which the difficulties, possibilities and limits of the broadcasting media could be effectively explained to the listening and viewing public. Until people are aurally and visually literate, they will be ill-equipped to criticise the way in which they are served and to discuss other ways of programme-making.

Style is also revealed in the posture, or stance, of the broadcasters. Technical tricks can shape the form programmes take, the way in which audiences are addressed — but they are not the only influence on broadcast manners. For example, the expectations of broadcasters and, certainly, of audiences are revealed in the types of programmes that predominate: in the 1940s and 1950s, 'talks' were fashionable; in the 1980s ''phone-ins'. Then there are linguistic habits. At one time those who gave the news announced or read it; the tone of voice in which they did so, the way in which they handled scripts, the absence of personal interpolation reminded the audience that the broadcasters merely delivered the news; they were not responsible for it. Now the news is presented. Those who deliver it may have written the script themselves; they are thought to be more closely engaged with the events they report. Another trend is towards couching programmes in popular speech, devising remarks that seek to reproduce natural conversation. The result is an uneasy hybrid, a fake demotic, that tries to bridge class and regional chasms and, simultaneously, to capture audiences by exploiting the differences between them.

Here is the first of the paradoxes. By trying to be real, the broadcasting organisations distort reality. Natural conversation, easy exchanges, accents out of the standard run, are extremely difficult to reproduce. Even worse, jocular familiarity, cosy confidences, can be profoundly annoying — alienating, not ingratiating. A second paradox is to be found in the attitudes of broadcasters themselves. There has begun to be a reaction against recent fashion. Certainly it is vital for radio and television to acquire and keep audiences but some who decide on policy or make programmes complain that stylistic standards of language and presentation have suffered in the process. A poor sort of popularity is bought at the cost of cheapening and trivialising what is offered. More, those who do so risk being disdainful towards the public; they are in danger of despising their audiences.

There are two other paradoxes. The first concerns intelligibility. By jettisoning its confident, precise, standard language and tone of voice, does a broadcasting service make its messages more easily understood, appreciated, remembered? Have broadcasters been so deeply hurt by allegations that their discourse is supercilious and superior that they have resorted to an incomprehensible and erratic babble? It takes more than 'ordinary' language and a 'democratic' manner, especially an odd approximation of these, to make programmes that are attractive and memorable. The easier the message is to grasp, the more effort has to be put into composing it.

And the last paradox? It is that 'style', something elusive, distinctive, special, is quickly reduced to 'formula', recognisable, reproducible, everyday. Broadcasting does not offer an exception to this tendency. The conference developed this thought when they came to discuss the remaining theme of the symposium: choice. Before that, though, it was necessary to examine the third aspect of style — prevailing assumptions.

These are revealed by the paradoxes. Obviously, it is easy to fall into the belief that in seeking popularity we are automatically striving for intelligibility. Clearly, too, we are inclined to be lazy and shy when it comes to thinking about popular usage, ordinary language, accents that give clues to the speaker's class, education, region or locality. We do not care to ask ourselves whose demotic we wish to foster, and why. Broadcasters assume that there is a close fit between the informal style adopted by the media and genuine popular speech. When this is not the case, the results sound patronising. Again, it is all too tempting for the broadcasters to avoid giving explanations of their own language and usages, to keep to themselves the technical and stylistic mysteries of their craft. They are encouraged in this by the fact that in Britain, as in many industrialised societies, there remains great reverence for the printed word above all other forms of communication. Society, the examination system, the universities, still stress the importance of literacy; visual, designing, engineering skills continue to be less enthusiastically espoused.

Less apparent, perhaps, are two other deficiencies in our thinking about broadcasting style. One is a failure to realise the connection between news stories and invented stories. The fiction to which audiences become attuned influences their reaction to fact: for example, the coincidence that the film *The China Syndrome* was released just before the accident at the Harrisburg nuclear power station demonstrated how profoundly an audience could be primed. And the reaction also goes in the other direction. News stories can be the source of popular mythologies; children, in particular, seize on reports of events as the foundation for elaborate, persistent and widespread fantasies. Historical events—the funerals of statesmen, political confrontations, papal enthronements, the death of kings — are popular dramas, corresponding to fictional stories and reinforcing our taste for them.

Another omission is our reluctance to admit that in adopting certain styles, postures, manners, we are conveying particular messages. Anthropologists remind us that a society's own style — of dress, ceremony, building, eating and drinking and so on — tells us not just about its attitudes to authority but also what is the structure of authority. Those who dominate impose their style, transmitting certain values throughout the society, and reinforcing the myths that correspond with those values. Style shows what choices a society cares, or is persuaded, to make.

Thus the symposium arrived at its third and last theme: choice, in relation to broadcasting. The symposium was first invited to consider a broadcasting system as a vital part of the whole communications network of a society, transmitting information and, in the words of Professor Deutsch's paper, facilitating the steering and self-steering of large groups of human beings. In thinking about the way to ensure autonomy, unpredictability, creativity, it is useful to draw on cybernetic theory. What is the memory upon which a broadcasting service depends? By what methods do broadcasters escape predictable ways of thinking and how are they encouraged to combine different sorts of information to produce unexpected insights and new knowledge? How are reactions fed back to the broadcasters, so that they discover how useful and how intelligible, or otherwise, the public has found their messages? All the responsibilities of a broadcasting system may be summed up in this way: that it should help a society to realise what it needs to know in order to create and survive.

To discharge this duty successfully is too great a task for a single system. The fewer the information-giving systems on which the public depends, the more uncritical citizens are likely to be. Messages may become distorted or soporific and there are no alternative channels from which to seek clarification or stimulus. It is also important for a broadcasting system itself, if it is to operate effectively, that there be rival services, offering different accounts and interpretations, presented in quite other styles. In Britain, for instance, the fact that the BBC and the IBA exist side by side enlivens the operation and performance of both services. The more channels of information a society has, the more creative the tension between them.

But this is the case, needless to say, only when the public is given real choice. If all the offerings are the same, the mere existence of a multiplicity of channels will not do very much to help society to learn, criticise, create, adapt. It was in this light that members of this symposium saw a subject which cannot be ignored: the survival of the BBC. Despite the promise of abundant, cheap and various broadcasting services, all conceived and ingeniously contrived,

,w technology, many fear that, during the next few years,
in British broadcasting will in fact be diminished. Though
:chnology does make some aspects of programme production
ι. umbersome, complicated and expensive, the costs of production do not fall, not least because fees, salaries and the price of
services continue to increase.

Broadcasting services which depend for their income on advertising revenue must compete ever more aggressively with each other,
to secure the audiences which attract the advertisers, and it is sport,
sex and entertainment that appeal to mass audiences. Presenting a
range and type of programmes that also attracts small, specialised
audiences and in which substantial amounts of more serious
material are offered becomes an increasingly costly exercise — but
this the British broadcasting services are obliged to do. The
'independent' programme companies are to a large extent cush-
ioned by their revenues; for the BBC, funded by a licence fee fixed
by the government, adaptation and survival is much more difficult,
especially when the licence fee is pitched low. The greater the
number of alternative services with which the BBC competes, the
more precarious its position. Staff and contributors are sucked away
to more lucrative employment, audiences decline and, so goes the
ominous prediction, those who settle the level of the licence fee find
it harder and harder to justify to themselves and to the public that
generous transfusions are needed.

The lessons of this discussion are these. First, more channels do
not necessarily offer wider choice. Competition between broadcasting companies induces each one to promote its own service more
and more vigorously. There is no countervailing effort: the public
does not exert counterbalancing authority and, for the most part,
does not appreciate how ruthless is the marketing onslaught to
which it is subjected. 'More choice' in fact means more
manipulation. From this, the symposium derived a second paradox:
that choice is not, after all, exercised most freely where there is no
guidance. We need to be educated in order to understand how our
choice is only superficially free and that we are on a leash of
influences, habits, addiction. To make choices, we need information
and, often, it has to be pressed upon us. It is this conundrum that the
British system of broadcasting regulation tries to answer, by leaving
the broadcasting authorities as unfettered as possible, while giving
certain guidelines, and by cherishing broadcasting services,
whether financed by advertising or out of the general revenue,

which at the same time answer popular demand and supply programmes that are unexpected, didactic or unpopular.

Can British broadcasting authorities continue to square the circle, to provide a 'public service' which does more than give the public what it wants? Only, members of the conference believed, if there is political commitment to this principle. The means exist by which the government exercises its authority and buttresses the broadcasters; the will is lacking to make effective use of these means. There are two reasons for this. In the first place it is unfashionable to admit to having any notion of what constitutes the public interest. To do so is to risk appearing narrow-minded and arrogant. Furthermore, it is in any case very difficult to settle on the nature of the public interest, even in the most general terms. But some general terms will help and they are also relevant where broadcasting is concerned: the public interest is served by systems which are informative and educative, which help a society to be cohesive and creative. The second reason why politicians and officials are reluctant to acknowledge commitment to public service broadcasting is because it is expensive, in money and in popularity. It is much less trouble simply to allow the market to run. But, as members of the symposium reminded each other, 'it all depends on how governments do their accounting'. The cost of shoring up a disintegrating, ill-informed, unadaptable citizenry far outweighs the cost of supporting effective, lively and innovative communications systems. And it is a grave mistake to assume that such support — moral as well as financial — can be given in a niggardly, grudging fashion. One tiny voice in the wilderness — one fragile service or part of a service — is easily drowned. The BBC, the IBA and any other public broadcasting authority that may be established needs to be allowed to thrive lustily — all of them. A certain critical mass is required to sustain creative enterprise.

Evidently, one tempting assumption is that the new broadcasting technology will of itself maximise public choice. On the contrary, it obliges us to think all the more carefully and inventively about systems of guidance and control. Another comfortable assumption is that those who watch and listen to television and radio can recognise and exercise choice. We should try to devise ways of helping them to do so and of minimising the circumstances in which choice is stifled. Nor should we rest in the happy belief that the broadcasting services Britain enjoys, and the systems that sustain them, offer the only models. They do not and, as it happens, they are themselves in some ways deficient. It was not only the foreign visitors at Leeds Castle who remarked on the predictability of the BBC's and independent companies' output, or who drew attention to the narrow definition of public service broadcasting still prevailing in this country (despite the strides made, for example, by local radio services). And the last, and the most useful, assumption? It is the belief that these knotty problems can be answered by categorising, labelling, quantifying. They cannot: not only is 'fiction' saturated with 'fact' — and vice versa — but 'entertainment' is loaded with 'information', including messages about power relationships — and vice versa. No single formula, no allocation of time, money, standing, will secure a perfect balance, define society's ideal communications system. Our arrangements and prescriptions must be makeshift and experimental. To work at all, a communications system needs to know how effectively it is performing and how it should adapt to changing circumstances, which, to some degree, have altered because of the system's own operation. In what ways, then, did members of the conference believe our broadcasting services should develop, particularly in Britain? And how did they suggest that such changes should be pressed? These were the remaining questions before the symposium. Let us take them one by one, under the three headings of authority, style and choice.

For the first, members of the conference believed that institutions are *charged* with authority, among them the government and the broadcasting organisations. Such authority is legitimate as long as those who exercise it are accountable and their efforts beneficial. Broadcasters must be committed to their role as publishers, reporting to the public. Respect for the individual utterance is vital to society and broadcasters must defend it, within broadcasting as elsewhere. And they should remember, always, the purpose of broadcasting: to try to discover whether society knows what it needs to know. Regulatory and licensing arrangements cannot by themselves ensure that broadcasting services are accountable and useful. Nor can new technology alone, however quickly it is developed and introduced. What is also required is sustained, creative thinking about attitudes and relationships: how tasks are assigned and co-ordinated, how different perspectives are introduced, how responses are assessed.

As for style, here too the symposium urged broadcasters to cherish openness and practicality. They should try to explain the grammar and usages of broadcasting, to make its mysteries explicit. Honesty about their own motives and methods is vital and the recognition that professionalism requires examination of standards and assumptions. Style, as much as content, helps to determine whether an audience is well or badly informed; without integrity and intelligibility, programmes are useless. Furthermore, a successful communications system also teaches people how to communicate with each other; the demotic that it fosters should not be that of one group only, whether drawn from the Establishment or from urban teenagers. Being understood is as important as understanding.

And choice? That is the most difficult of all. Legitimate authority will always be besieged by the fraudulent and trivial. A certain strength is enjoyed by those who are open to criticism, honest about their own motives, necessary because they acquire and transmit knowledge. But they are also at a disadvantage, because their messages may not be immediately attractive to an insecure and thirsty public and because, whatever the long-term value of those messages and the organisations that carry them, the price seems high and it has to be paid now. So what should be done if, as members of the symposium believed, public service broadcasting is essential for the well-being, creativity and, ultimately, freedom and survival of society? Those who are responsible for broadcasting will have to think strategically. The introduction of new technology and new opportunities must not be handled vaguely and haphazardly, but as astutely and in as ordered a manner as possible. It is also vital to think politically: how best can accountability and independence be blended and protected? What new relationships can be devised between the government, the broadcasters and the public? What experiments will be tried in the form and language of programming? How can tastes be widened, cultural and intellectual challenges be made attractive? In these three questions, the themes of the symposium are brought together; they were not solved, but to ask them is at least a beginning.

Richard Hoggart

Closing Observations

The major theme we started with and kept coming back to was 'authority' and especially, though not only, authority in broadcasting. It is worth recalling that broadcasting is the one medium of communication on which all nation states took conscious thought before they set up systems. The first reason for this was that resources were limited, channels were limited; by comparison, printing outlets are potentially infinite. So governments had to decide in advance; but of course *how* they decided to set up broadcasting, how they financed it, what structures they gave it, reflected the different natures of different societies. Many wanted to keep their hands on it, to be able to censor it; but the universally applicable reason for governmental intervention from the start was shortage of resources. Yet it is now possible to say that that shortage is about to disappear — this is why we are all aware of being at a kind of watershed.

Around the idea of authority an extraordinary set of words has been circling in our discussions. One has been half-hiding and has popped out only now and again. This is 'consensus'. In the debate about broadcasting 'consensus' has by now become a slightly dirty word. It's 'the consensus' which the BBC assumes and, according to some writers about broadcasting, rams down our throats relentlessly. So the word which largely took its place in this debate was 'coherence'. It was argued that British society *does* have a certain coherence and that this should be reflected by the broadcasters; that the people who have the 'authority', whether they are members of the supervisory bodies or broadcasters, make legitimate and reinforce the values (often unspoken) of the assumed 'coherence'. I believe there is a sense in which that is true. The BBC especially, for historic and other reasons, does appear to speak for the nation on certain occasions. It comes over in tone of voice or the whole way in which an event is approached as much as in *what* is said. The Corporation assumes it *knows* the country and its sense of values. I don't think this is always regrettable or mistaken. But the BBC does walk on the water sometimes and takes a great deal for granted in the way of unspoken assumptions. It was argued here that we hand over the 'authority' for thus enforcing this 'coherence' to a group who then become — in a different sense of the word — the voice of Authority. In other countries, someone said, governments had to legislate for every item of good behaviour in broadcasting. How useful, therefore, that here we can assume the ability to select certain people who will have the sense of the 'coherence' of this society in the right ways without necessarily ever actually articulating it. I believe they are called 'the great and the good' and that they are on a list somewhere. The questions which lurk behind it are: does such a group in fact select only one highly contingent set of values? Does it, through the sense of itself carrying this burden, deny certain diversities in this society? Does it thin out the culture; does it make us appear less plural than we are and less divided? My answer would be that it does these things very often. I have always liked a BBC phrase to defend its newly-found aggressiveness in the 1960s. I think Oliver Whitley may have invented it: 'Good broadcasting shows the quarrel of a society with itself'.

I am willing to argue that the interesting ways in which broadcasting, national broadcasting, does give us a sense of national coherence are less significantly seen on such occasions as Churchill's funeral or the Cup Final than in — say — broadcast comedy. Some of the best comedy programmes have made this society laugh all the way through; and this we would never have found out if broadcasters hadn't gone out on a limb to make those programmes.

But to return to 'the authorities'. Where exactly does their authority come from? In what sense are they 'accountable' (another of the recurrent words)? We were told this morning that they should be more publicly visible so that they could be criticised more. We all want that, but it is in fact difficult to bring about in a useful way. Public sessions are by now quite fashionable among public bodies — the IBA, the BBC and now the Arts Council practise them. The ones I have experienced are usually no better than the disease they seek to cure; they do not increase real accountability. The Arts Council's public sessions tend to attract almost entirely individuals or groups all of whom want more money than they are getting; the air is heavy with the smell of axes being ground. The officials look longingly for one ordinary citizen who is a customer of Arts Council-supported activities. There rarely is one, because the two hundred tickets have been snapped up weeks in advance by the 105-Piccadilly-watchers. The IBA is, though, accountable to Parliament since it was established by Act; the BBC, being established by Royal Charter, isn't. Ah, we are then usually told, but the BBC has over the decades built up case-law for its own behaviour, a sort of tradition of public accountability which is passed on from governor to governor and Director-General to Director-General. Maybe. But one can't help marvelling at their assurance; and one remembers that famous remark to the effect that, if Genghis Khan became chairman of the BBC, within six months he'd be a staunch supporter of the institution and its mores.

I hope you'll excuse my frequent references to the Arts Council, but I think the comparisons can be interesting. The Arts Council is, compared with the BBC, a relatively young organisation, at least in its present scope. Its large funds have arrived only in the last fifteen years or so. It still lacks adequate case-law and established practice, adequate, that is, to the immense pressures on it. So it quickly betrays nervousness and acts jumpily. The Community Arts people lean on it one way and make it feel guiltily élitist, and the four great national companies — the Royal Opera House, English National Opera, the National Theatre and the Royal Shakespeare Company — lean on it the other way and remind them that 'Art must be kept up' and at the highest level. So the Council tends to ricochet, for want of a thought-out set of positions.

But the most obvious comparison with the BBC must be with commercial television and radio. For me these discussions have underlined the view that the IBA — which has a lot to its credit — is hobbled. It is hobbled because it is inorganic to broadcasting. It is separated from programme-making, is regulatory at a distance — and therefore it has to be retrospective or it will become too interfering, a pre-censor too often (it sometimes is). It is, as it were, working against the grain, because it has been set up to *overlook* broadcasting from outside, is not in the day-to-day business and battle of making programmes, in the discussions, the costings, the sense of what the programme-makers are trying to do and say, the clash of artists with planners, of formal policy with invention.

So how, some of us have kept asking, do you find 'authorities' other than 'the great and the good'? In the jargon of cultural debate today this is known as 'democratising' the BBC governors, the IBA or the Arts Council. I think the word 'democratise' can be a confusing placebo in this context. But that is another story. For it is true that the range from which such people are drawn is too narrow and the procedures still too ingrown. I have heard the chairman of a national body say he thought Mrs So-and-So would make a splendid member. I wondered on what he based the view and discovered that he'd found her a lively companion at a dinner party some nights before. Things are changing, if very slowly. Names for the membership of new national councils are now often trawled-for both publicly and privately and therefore more widely than they used to be. It never ceases to amaze me that in response to public advertisement a great many people propose themselves.

Unfortunately, most proposals for improving the system are formalistic and unreal, populist rather than democratic. For instance — to turn to the Arts Council yet again — a Labour Party committee proposed a mandated council of people elected, all over the country, from local authorities and unions and the like. Apart from being likely to produce a worse council than the present system, this one would result in giving far too much power to the Chairman and the Secretary General. I'm not saying there can't be a way other than such extremes; I think there could be. But it will be likely to be a mixed way. There is no simple solution, and to use words like 'democratic' as a slogan is merely to blur the issue.

We also talked a great deal about the 'authority' of the broadcasters themselves as contrasted with that of their supervisory bodies. One of us remarked on how the broadcasters' tones have changed in twenty years; from, as it were, sensing themselves as those who hand down certain values through their whole style to their becoming echo-sounders of the vast deeps of society, feeding back those echoes of change into the corporation. It was a nice image and goes a long way.

We didn't, and such a meeting in any other society I know of would not have been able to make such an omission, much refer to censorship. That's chiefly because overt censorship hardly exists. What we didn't go into, though, and in fact we rather skirted away from it, is the unspoken 'coherence-editing or consensus–editing' which certainly does go on. If you say this to broadcasters they become unhappy or angry. I thought the largely antagonistic reaction of the broadcasters to the book *Bad News*[1] was extreme. No doubt the book's sociological apparatus could be criticised, but the central point it is making — about unconscious editing of many kinds — was not fully taken by most broadcasters. I remember being part of a television discussion of the book, with — among others — a distinguished television newsman. He simply couldn't see the point. He kept saying: but there is 'the news' out there and we are giving it to you. It was graspable. These issues came up obliquely in our discussions here, in references to the importance of not throwing the baby out with the bath water, of not saying: because there is this kind of unconscious selection in editing there is no such thing as objectivity; it's not worth going for. Of course there's no such thing as absolute objectivity; but there is the *effort* at objectivity, which some of us make better and some worse. We do better to the extent that we are aware of our own inbuilt assumptions; which is why I think it is important that books such as *Bad News* are written, and are talked about among broadcasters.

Behind all this there is, in turn, the question of English voices. As our discussion went on I realised afresh how full the English language is of phrases which indicate that we are deeply concerned about the way we speak to one another. Phrases such as 'Who do you think you're talking to?' which is a staple British expression and has a whole range of assumptions about class and hierarchy and superiorities within it; or 'Don't use that tone of voice with me' which almost always comes out at critical moments in arguments. I constantly find myself saying: 'What kind of people do they think we are?' when I hear broadcasters using some kinds of language or tone. Yet I believe broadcasting at its best has made a real gain in demotic communication. There is a good sense in which it has occasionally made us feel as one nation. Still, more and more — and this was another of our recurrent themes — more and more it is avoiding formal styles of 'English' communication. The results are sometimes horrendous, in phoney, mid-Atlantic mélanges. Though, if you move out of the central areas of broadcasting into the fringe areas, especially the fringe specialist areas, you can make some wonderful finds. If you switch on Radio 4 at about six in the morning you hear people across the nation quoting at each other the prices of lamb and potatoes and beef in their areas, and they never alter their native accents. Glasgow comes up rich and strong and then Swansea and then Lincolnshire; they know what they are talking about; they're not having to aim at a central audience; they're speaking directly to a specialist audience, and no translation is needed. It's a lovely programme, and reminds us how complex is the tapestry of British voices and how rarely we even now trust ourselves to release them on radio and television. Semi-artificial 'central' voices, plus the permitted range of 'odd' other accents, are more the pattern.

When I was an extra-mural tutor back in 1948 I had a class in Goole which included three grammar school teachers' wives. The university department lent me one of those new-fangled things called a tape-recorder, since I thought it would be useful to tape part of a discussion so as to show how we wandered all over the place. When the tape was played back the three ladies were clearly embarrassed. They had heard their own voices for the first time. They were Yorkshire women and therefore the ribs of their voices were basic Yorkshire — flat vowels, in particular. But their voices were also those of grammar school teachers' wives. They had a slightly educated, almost genteel, modulation in their voices. What they themselves heard in their heads was this posher sound, quite distinct from the usual Goole voice. But when the recording was played back the great Yorkshire ribs of their voices came through, and they felt ashamed. I was surprised and very sorry, too, to have exposed them without warning to that shock. They didn't come to the class again. They insisted that the machine had distorted their voices. I don't think it had. It was they who were used to tuning into only that aspect of their speech which differentiated it from that of the Goole people around them.

About 'choice' we talked a great deal, about how far most of us want to extend our choices and how far we don't; and by what right anyone presumes to try to do that. One of the virtuous guiding assumptions of the BBC especially has been that broadcasters have a duty to help inform our choices, make them wider than they are at present, put different tastes before us. Yet we don't really know how far broadcasters *do* thus affect us, do make us 'surprised by joy' by new things which we'd never otherwise have thought of and so become interested in. Yet the assumption seems fair if you look at the great range of subjects now enjoying success on television.

In this whole part of our discussions we touched on one aspect quite often, and almost wholly ignored another. We talked a good deal about 'reinforcement' through broadcasting, through current affairs, plays, situation comedies and almost anything else. We talked about broadcasting's tendency to legitimate authority. We heard almost nothing about what audiences *take* from programmes, what they *do* with them; about what happens inside individuals.

There is a useful comparison with literary criticism of popular fiction here. Early criticism tended to assume that what an educated reader found in popular fiction — the conventional, trite and stereotyped — exactly reflected the lives of those who read it, that there was an unselective and uncritical match between books and readers. It was C. S. Lewis who, surprisingly, first persuaded me (through his writing; I did not know him) that people can take good things from very poor literature, that they can select from it rather than being victims of it. George Orwell was on to the same argument. It puts the debate into another perspective but, so far as I know, has not been adequately followed through in writing about either literature or broadcasting. We touched too lightly, too, on the *nature* — not only the justification — of the creative intervention in broadcasting by authors and producers. About this whole area one always remembers: 'How do I know what I think till I see what I say?'. For broadcasting this runs 'How do I know what I like till I see what it's possible to have?'. The world is a good deal wider than any of us think and so we ought to be offered the chance to widen our tastes.

In all this the underlying main question is: What is the role of broadcasters in the process of social change? We tend often to overestimate it and then, in reaction, to dismiss it. It would be particularly useful to examine the place of broadcasting in relation to the great secular changes in 'style' in Britain during the 1960s. How far were they going on all the time underneath? Did broadcasting initiate or simply reflect? And by reflecting did it hasten? We do not know. Someone asked me the other day to sum up the 'liberating effect' of the *Lady Chatterley's Lover*[2] trial. But I think that trial was, at the most, catalytic of changes which were going on anyway; or perhaps less than that — a *post facto* symbolic moment. Apparently the chief prosecuting counsel was surprised and shocked that anyone would use *that* word in a book: the judge too looked baffled; perplexed in the extreme. He simply didn't know that people wrote and read books like that; and he did seem to think that ordinary people were going to come to an awful pass if the book were let loose on them. But we know that when the book was read in a room at the back of the Old Bailey by the jurors a majority of them asked what all the fuss was about. This was even before the trial had started. Large changes had been under way which the 'authorities' had not noticed.

Here is another example. I have quoted it elsewhere but think it relevant enough to bear repetition here. When I went to Birmingham in the early 1960s the university had just acquired a barber's shop. Quite soon it was discovered by the authorities that the barber, as barbers have done from time immemorial, was selling French letters, contraceptives, sheaths. This so shocked the powers that be that he was told to leave. The popular press had a front page lead about the dreadful fact that contraceptives had been on sale on a campus. Only two or three years later one of my students became pregnant. I went to see the university doctor to discuss it with him, at her request. On the counter of the reception area I noticed, whilst I was waiting to be seen, a box full of little packets. I asked the nurse whether they were what was called 'the pill' and she said yes. So you just hand them out? Well, they have to tell us they are having a serious relationship, she said. So big a change in so few years! What was the place of broadcasting in articulating and encouraging such changed attitudes? I am one of those who think it probably played an important part. As I've said, it's a pity we don't *know* more, since these changes in the 1960s are probably the most important changes of attitude to have occurred in this century. They could be fairly reliably analysed. Instead of doing that, we tend to make superficial remarks about the Beatles, Lady Chatterley and liberation by the pill.

One of the attitudes which almost always appears in discussions about broadcasting (though it hasn't been evident in our discussions) is a deepseated *protectiveness* towards audiences. British authorities are generally, traditionally, deeply cautious about what 'ordinary' people can take. One remembers again the Lady Chatterley trial and that famous question by the prosecuting counsel which seemed incredible even then: would you (the jury) wish your wives and servants to read this book? It was said seriously by a man who apparently was 'a decent sort of chap' but, again, perplexed. The hidden assumption, the hidden frame for the agenda, is that we must temper the wind to the shorn lambs; and that they are all pretty well shorn. At its best, broadcasting in Britain has rejected this point of view and as a result has shown that we are more intelligent, more imaginative than might be thought, especially as might be thought from a glance at the popular press, particularly today.

All these elements, as they've woven in and out of the discussion, have emphasised yet again the importance of an interdisciplinary approach in studies of broadcasting. There have been representatives of several disciplines here, especially the sociological and the literary; and those make a good basic pair. There is obviously a place for discussing broadcasting *systems*, as we have been doing. But most discussions about the nature and quality of broadcasting suffer because they do not start by looking at the-thing-in-itself, by a response to actual programmes, their inwardness, stance, relation to their genre and all that. It is usually best to start there, with 'style', before moving into questions of structure, of authority, power and choice.

Another aspect we only lightly, far too lightly, touched on is international comparisons. The general assumption has been that most societies are rather like ours. Yet they simply aren't. We did hear, from a participant from another continent, a clear statement of a different way of looking at, of seeing, yourself as a broadcaster — in his case as precisely the carrier of the message of the authority which is outside, that of the government. We British have in our bones the notion of the broadcaster as an active intervener, with editorial standards and a distance from any dictation. When this other point of view was being put one of the British bobbed up immediately and said 'Still, if they [the government] give you a text for the news, you can always put your own oar in'. That remark would be incomprehensible or explosive in many countries. In those places they haven't *got* oars; they don't expect to have any; and if they made some and 'put them in' they would immediately be in serious trouble with the authorities.

Early in my time at UNESCO there was a great fuss because the Soviet authorities had refused to give Rostropovich an external visa to go to (I think it was) Yehudi Menuhin's festival at Gstaad. I was asked to intervene. An official was going to Moscow so I asked him to speak about the matter to Madame Furtseva, the Minister of Culture. She wasn't available·so he saw her deputy, Popov. The UNESCO official explained Mr Menuhin's concern and that of the International Council of Music. He suggested that the incident might have a bad effect on the Moscow meeting of ICM, which was to be held in a few months. Popov, he said, was amazed at the intervention. He stood stock still in the corridor and his eyes widened (he is huge, and usually wears one of those black double-breasted suits which make men look as if they have been poured into them). He uttered one word, the Russian equivalent of 'merde'. He couldn't, said my emissary, he simply couldn't, conceive the notion of an individual saying 'I object to that' about a governmental decision. There was no room for dialogue, there was no way for talking; the situation was beyond comprehension for him — that an individual could react thus and expect to be heard. So we have to recognise that you can't 'put your oar in', in most societies, if you are a broadcaster. But we have, as if in our blood, the idea that broadcasting has something to do with us as *choosing* individuals, that it has something to do with our 'quarrels with society'. All this side of things our discussions hardly touched on.

Some interesting things were said about the relationship of broadcasters to other cultures; but there is not time to recapitulate those. And we glanced at the likely effect of new technologies. We are being told that many new kinds of broadcasting, more plural broadcasting, will be possible. The old regulatory structure will not be able to cope. Here again and rather too quickly words such as 'access', 'participation', 'democratic broadcasting' are in fashion. Fine: but we ought also to think about what may be at risk. In a recent paper an IBA senior official said bleakly that the new technologies will 'give us more broadcasting, much more — but it will be worse'.

I think he was foreseeing several risks and losses. First, with so much available we will tend to choose our programmes according to our *existing* tastes, we will be less likely to be taken by surprise, to widen our taste or think again. We will know *our* kind of channel. In a way we do that today, but not so much. And there will be less likelihood of coming together nationally in what I called the better sense — in enjoying a comedy show, for instance.

One of the great virtues of British broadcasting at present is not so much Radio 3 — good though that is. It is Radio 4, and for this reason: if you listen to Radio 4 over a week you realise how it provides for a patchwork of genuine minority needs which have no political clout, such as those of the disabled, the old, the bedridden, etc. All this is a product of the present, protected, semi-paternalism and arises from the idea of a national broadcasting responsibility, a national duty, from the idea of broadcasters not being so harried by money problems or audience problems that they can't afford such care for minorities. That is another of the things which will be at risk if broadcasting is thrown wholly into the open market.

Above all, a broadcasting authority should be a fifth estate. I don't think it will be claiming too much if it aims at that. It should have enough size and weight and mass to be able to be a force any government has to reckon with, a critical force which politicians and other powers must take account of and know is watching them. If you split the system into a range of different units catering for different existing tastes you will take away the broadcaster's capacity to arrive at that kind of 'authority' (in yet another sense of that word).

My impression is that politicians in general are not yet aware of these issues. If they become interested in them, they tend to become, quite simply, technologically fascinated. Industrialists are aware of what the profits may be. We are not very good as a nation at having public debates about these sorts of thing, about policy implications, the best use of the media, i.e. their relation to the quality of our lives. If we don't have a national debate about this one pretty soon nobody is going to be adequately informed; and thus choices will be made for us by default.

NOTES

1. *Bad News*, Glasgow University Media Group (Routledge and Kegan Paul, London, 1976).
2. The novel by D. H. Lawrence, published by Penguin in 1960, after an unsuccessful injunction had been sought by the Director of Public Prosecutions.

Index

advertisements, 46, 71
Advertising Standards Authority, 24
Advisory Committee on Spoken English, 82, 96
Agnew, Spiro, 27–8
Alan, A. J., 87
All in the Family, 119
Allen, Jim, 48
American Broadcasting Corporation, 131–2
Annan Committee on the Future of Broadcasting (Chairman, Lord Annan): on ideal of public service, 1; description of broadcasting, 5; and collection of licence fees, 5; on cohesive power of broadcasting, 16; on news and documentary programmes, 37; on responsibility for broadcasting, 42, 52; on broadcasting Authorities, 45, 52; and spoken English, 95; on influence of TV, 97
announcers, 39, 84; *see also* language
anonymity, 29–30
Archers, The, 16, 121
Aristotelian Society, *Proceedings*, 32
Army Game, The, 42
Arts Council, 151–3
Associated Television (ATV), 45, 52
audience research, 110
Australia, 54
authority: changing role of, 20–5, 39–40; and monopoly, 22; defined and identified, 25–7, 30–1, 134–5; dissent and challenge to, 27, 32; exercise of, 31–2, 42, 45, 49–51; 'crisis of', 32, 35; attitude of broadcasters to, 33–7, 137; and hierarchy, 50–1; political, 54, 136; and bureaucrats, 58–9; and communications system, 104; indi-

vidual and class attitudes to, 109–13; and types of drama, 125; and style, 133; as theme, 134, 150, 153; and balance, 137, 139; and choice, 140; and power, 140–1; legitimacy of, 148–9
Avengers, The, 118
Aylestone, Herbert William Bowden, Baron, 45

Bad News (Glasgow Media Group publication), 153–4
balance of authority, 137, 139
Barnum, Phineas T., 42
Begin, Menachem, 54
Bernstein, Cecil, 42
Bernstein, Sidney Lewis, Baron, 42–4
Bevin, Ernest, 14
Biddulph, Jim, 90, 92
Black Beauty, 119
Black, Peter, 87
Blake, William, 22, 26
Bonanza, 127
Bond, Edward, 51
Bond, James, 128–9
Bostock, Tom, 93
bribery, 9
Briggs, Asa, Baron, 35, 64–5
British Broadcasting Corporation (BBC): conflicting ideals in, 1; praised, 1–2; staff losses, 1–2; overseas and external services, 2, 11; competition from independent companies, 3, 38, 145–6; financing and licence revenues, 5–6, 71–2, 146; staff appointments, 7; monopoly broken, 22–3; charter, 22, 152; status, 26; governing of, 35; role of Chairman, 35; responsibility of